Hil
Sout
We

30 Walking Routes in Beara and surrounding areas

DAVID HERMAN

SHANKSMARE PUBLICATIONS

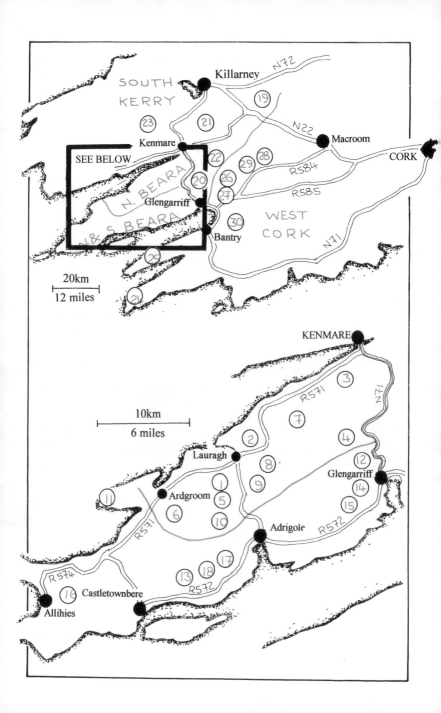

SOUTH KERRY

Killarney

N72

N22

Macroom

CORK

Kenmare

SEE BELOW

N. BEARA

N. & S. BEARA

Glengarriff

Bantry

RS84

RS85

WEST CORK

N71

20km
12 miles

KENMARE

R571

N71

Lauragh

Ardgroom

R571

Glengarriff

R572

Adrigole

R574

R572

Castletownbere

Allihies

10km
6 miles

CONTENTS

A Quick Look Around; How to Use this Book; Getting to the Region; Getting Around the Region; Accommodation; Maps; Long Distance Paths; A Few Route Selections; Safety; What to Carry with you; Rights of Way and Good Conduct; They're your Mountains too - Get Involved!; Useful Contacts.

* *Routes with major variations, most of them shorter than the main route*

A QUICK LOOK AROUND

The region covered by this book is primarily the Beara Peninsula (specifically the area west of the N71), but also the smaller peninsulas to its south, the area round Kenmare at the south of the Iveragh Peninsula, and the region of west Cork inland of the Beara Peninsula. By the way, I do not use the terms usually given to the mountain ranges in this region (Caha Mountains, Shehy Mountains etc). This is simply because this is not the way I have divided up the routes. No slight intended.

I have to admit that when I started research for this book I had little idea of what the region had to offer, though I can fairly claim to have a good knowledge of nearly every other mountain range in the country. This was partly because of the region's distance from my base in Dublin; it must be the most distant part of the country to reach from the capital. In addition, if one is travelling to the south-west one first encounters the superb ranges of the Dingle and Iveragh peninsulas. Why travel any further?

Well, now I know why. The region covered by this book is magnificent: marvellous peaks, wild and remote mountain valleys, lonely tarns and memorable sea-cliffs. It's a great area for hill-walking. But why not see for yourself?

Let's look at the entire region, here divided into four areas, in a little more detail. Probably the most rugged area is **North Beara**, the part of Beara in county Kerry. Apart from the well-known Cummeengeera Circuit, there several walks in the immediate area which are almost as good. In **West and South Beara** one major target is Hungry Hill, which may also be climbed, though more hazardously, from the north. It and the characteristic cone of Sugar Loaf are the main goals in this area, though there are a series of generally lower peaks reaching westward to the end of the peninsula, which offer excellent walking.

South Kerry, as arbitrarily defined by this book, covers the fairly small area of the county not covered by *Hill Walkers Kerry*, the companion volume to this one. It therefore includes the southern approaches to some of the high peaks of the magnificent Iveragh mountains as well as little-known but excellent hill walking areas to their east. **West Cork**, as well as including lovely sea cliff walking, encompasses remote and rugged mountains and also gently-moulded hills that merge into rich undulating farm country to their east.

HOW TO USE THIS BOOK

First of all, it is only fair to state that a map is needed in order to walk most of the routes in this book. More about suitable maps is given below and with each route description.

I have tried to cover all the best and most characteristic of the mountain areas in the region. Since the most characteristic are not necessarily the best, there had to be some compromises in choosing routes. As always in this series I have taken a 'warts and all' approach; that is I do not describe everywhere and every route as being superlatively good. However it has to be said that this region has a bewildering array of superlatively good mountains to walk and a choice was difficult. All routes detailed here have more than a few favourable characteristics but some are better than others. My opinions are simply that - opinions - and yours might well be quite different.

The Sketch Maps: These accompany all route descriptions and are sufficient for the easier walks only. Their aim is to emphasise what is *not* on the maps: cliffs, walls, fences etc. In particular they show roughly the location of long lines of sandstone slabs, a feature that is almost unique to this area of Ireland and that can result in very slow progress. Features that are important for navigation or reassurance are shown in red. All these maps, except those for routes 20, 25 and 26, which are on a slightly smaller scale to fit them onto the page, are on a scale of 1:50 000, that is the same as the Ordnance Survey (OS) maps. North is always to the top of the page. The symbols are explained on the inside back cover.

Before you set off on a walk it might be a good idea to pencil in the proposed route onto your map from the sketch map.

Grid References: These are the four- or six-digit numbers preceded by the letters 'GR', which appear after some locations, particularly the starting points of routes. The figure uniquely identifies the location on most maps. The system is explained on all OS maps.

The following notes refer to each of the paragraphs that form the route description for each route.

'Getting There': To get to the starting point of many of these routes involves miles of travel on bad minor, and nearly as bad, major roads. There's more about this in 'Getting Around the Region' below.

'Walking Time': This time is based on a variation of Naismith's Rule. It allows one hour for 4km on the flat plus one hour for each 500m of climbing. Thus a walk of 2km on the flat with a climb of 250m should take 1 hour. This is a fairly leisurely pace but it does not allow much time for eating, taking photographs or any other normal stops. Where justified this walking time is adjusted for difficult terrain (eg steep descents, rough vegetation) or easy terrain (eg tracks). There are some sections of some routes, particularly where slabs have to be negotiated (either uphill or down), where it is difficult to be even roughly accurate as to how long it will take to walk. These sections are noted in the 'Walking Time' paragraph.

'Difficulties': This is mostly self-explanatory, but note that wet ground can make routes much more difficult, especially routes that involve scrambling or clambering over rocks. Heavy rain might make streams which are normally fordable completely impassable.

'Map' gives the best map(s) for the route. Where one is specified it is advisable that it be taken. There is more about suitable maps below.

'Route': The place names used here (and elsewhere) are those used on the OS Discovery Series maps regardless of whether they are the commonly used versions. The one major exception is Castletownbere (Castletownberehaven on the maps) both because this is the name usually used and because its shortened form is already long enough.

GETTING TO THE REGION

BY CAR

In trying to describe how to get by car to the region covered by this book I was faced by a basic problem. This is that while the Beara Peninsula is a compact area of mountains, the remainder of the region is quite diffuse and the mountain ranges scattered. With this in mind I have taken three centres and describe below how to get to each. These are Killarney, which is convenient to parts of south Kerry and west Cork; Kenmare, which is the largest town close to the Beara Peninsula; and Glengarriff which is also close to the Beara Peninsula but is in addition a gateway to much of south-west Cork. Note that all three towns are connected by short stretches of the N71 through rugged mountain country and that both Killarney and Kenmare are also excellent centres for extensive mountain areas covered by *Hill Walkers Kerry*.

From Dublin to **Killarney** the shortest route is along the N7 to Limerick, here take the N20 and then the N21 from where the route is well signposted. **Kenmare** can also be reached from Killarney over the N71. Alternatively to get from Dublin to Kenmare you can take N8 to Fermoy, the N72 to near Killarney, the N22 for a short distance and then the R569 to Kenmare. Kenmare may also be reached from Cork by taking the N22 to near Macroom, here branching onto the R584 to near **Glengarriff** and from there taking a slow section of the N71 to Kenmare. You are unlikely to make high speeds on any section of road in the south-west of the country.

BY PUBLIC TRANSPORT

The nearest train stations to the region are Killarney and Cork, which have connections to Dublin. The nearest airport is at Farranfore, between Killarney and Tralee. Shannon and Cork airports are further away.

The following Bus Eireann services (☎ 064-34777) are *express*, that is they stop only in designated towns. The timetable 40 service runs from Rosslare Harbour through Cork and Macroom and thence north-west through Millstreet and Killarney. The 50 and a sub-route of the 40 run from Cork through Macroom and Ballyvourney to Killarney. The 42 runs from Cork to Macroom and thence north-west through Millstreet and Killarney. The 44 and 46 take a more southerly route from Cork through Bandon with the 44 reaching Kenmare and Killarney (over a mountainous section of the N71) and the 46 reaching Castletownbere in Beara and the end of the Mizen peninsula.

Note that local bus services (outlined below) might also be used to get into the region.

GETTING AROUND THE REGION

BY CAR

The principal road along the northern side of the Beara Peninsula is the R571, which runs from Kenmare to Castletownbere. On the southern side of the peninsula the R572 runs from Glengarriff to Castletownbere. Both these roads give a good idea of the type of mountain terrain you may expect in Beara.

However for a really close-up idea take the Healy Pass Road (R574) which runs from Lauragh to Adrigole and reaches 290m in crossing Beara's mountain range. On the northern side the road gives excellent views to the mountains of Cummeengeera (route 1, 5). On the winding southern side there are marvellous glimpses of the mountains around Adrigole.

In the part of this book not covering the Beara Peninsula, the N71 pursues a scenic but leisurely course south from Glengarriff along the coast of west Cork. At Ballylickey (between Glengarriff and Bantry) the R584 heads for Macroom and it and the R585, which diverges from it, both cross scenic passes at Keimaneigh and Cousane, the first of these leading to mountain country around Gougane Barra. However, if you want a walk-free introduction to the mountains of this area take the unclassified road from Ballylickey to Kilgarvan, which will take about an hour. The road reaches 380m and will give you an excellent idea of the rugged country covered by routes 22 and 26.

A comparatively fast road, the N22, runs from Killarney to Cork. Branching from it are the N72 which runs parallel to the Paps and the mountains to its east and the R569, a slow but scenic road running through mountain country to Kenmare.

BY BUS

The following Bus Eireann services are *local*, that is they stop anywhere it is safe to do so. Timetable 270 runs from Killarney through Kilgarvan (ie *not* along the mountainous N71) and thence along the southern side of Iveragh. The 282, a most useful service for walkers, runs from Kenmare along the northern side of the Beara Peninsula and thence into Castletownbere. Further inland the 230 runs from Cork through Macroom to Ballyvourney with a sub-route branching south to Ballingeary. Lastly the 255 (a Saturday only service) runs from Macroom through Ballingeary to Kilcrohane near the end of the Sheep's Head peninsula. A private firm, Harrington's (☎ 027-74003) runs a service from Castletownbere east along the R572 to Glengarriff (and Cork) in the mornings and returns in the evenings. You should book this service a day or two in advance.

If you are relying solely on public transport the best place to stay to explore the region is undoubtedly Kenmare. From there you can get a bus fairly early in the morning along the north side of the Beara Peninsula and walk east to pick up the return bus in the evening. From Castletownbere you can also use the 282 service (less usefully than if you were based in Kenmare) or Harrington's buses to explore the mountains on the south of the peninsula.

BY COACH OR TAXI

If you are a large party it may be more economical to use a coach or taxi rather than public transport. The firms providing such services are listed in the golden pages of the telephone directory.

BY BICYCLE

There are several places where bikes may be hired and you will find the current list in the golden pages of the telephone directory. Don't forget that, if you have only one car, you can use a bike to make A to B walks. As well as arranging that A and B are not too far apart, try to ensure that the bike journey will not be all uphill and that you are not cycling into the prevailing westerly winds.

HITCHHIKING

This is a time-honoured way of getting round all over rural Ireland. However, if you are dripping wet and carrying a bulky rucksack your chances will not be enhanced. Of course, this is just the time you will really want a lift! Women travelling alone after dark should avoid hitching.

ACCOMMODATION

Let's look at the Beara Peninsula first.

Kenmare, an attractive little town (big for this area) has, as noted above a fairly good bus service and is a good centre for exploring the mountains of south Iveragh and north Beara. **Lauragh** (particularly), **Tuosist** or **Ardgroom** are all small villages and are ideal for exploring the most attractive areas of Beara. **Glengarriff** is much bigger than the three villages just mentioned and is a good centre for the southern side of Beara and for the mountains to its east. **Castletownbere** is fairly well situated for the mountains on the south side of the Beara Peninsula.

For the remainder of south Kerry and west Cork, it is unlikely that you will be specifically trying to explore the mountains from one or even several centres since the mountain ranges are small and scattered and the road system does not facilitate it. It is much more likely that you will use larger centres that can also be used for mountain ranges not covered by this book, and face a longer car journey to explore them. With this in mind, **Killarney** is well located for the mountains to its east as well as its west. **Glengarriff, Kilgarvan** and **Bantry** (as well as Kenmare mentioned above) are fairly large towns and good centres though inevitably remote from some mountain areas while **Ballingeary** and **Kealkill** are smaller centres for more localised areas.

MAPS

The OS's up-to-date 1:50 000 Discovery Series covers the region more than adequately. Sheet 78 covers the area north of Kenmare and sheet 79 the area to its north-east. The Beara Peninsula is covered on sheets 84 and 85 with the latter also covering much of the non-peninsular west Cork. Sheet 88 covers the smaller, southerly peninsulas.

Since most hill walkers will use the Discovery Series sheets it is worthwhile pointing out a few of their more important characteristics.

- Cliffs are not explicitly depicted, so you must use your judgement by noting the convergence of contour lines. Contour lines have been omitted altogether in the case of some sections of sea-cliff.
- Forests tend not to be as extensive as depicted.
- Many firebreaks are shown as forest tracks. In general, 'tracks' shown on the maps which ignore the lie of the land and are shown traversing hill and valley in straight lines are in fact firebreaks. Actual tracks tend to keep to gentle slopes and to wind in zig-zag fashion on steep ones.
- The thin black or grey lines shown in some upland areas are field boundaries of some kind, usually walls or earthbanks.
- Few paths or footbridges are shown. The long distance paths are badly depicted in places.
- The thickness of the lines used to indicate streams usually has little bearing on how wide they actually are. In mountain areas, except after heavy rain, it is usually possible to ford streams.

Other maps may be dealt with more briefly. The old half-inch to the mile (1:126 720) series is no longer published, though you may be able to buy copies of the relevant sheet 24, and of 20 and 21, both of which are of marginal interest. These maps are of use in getting to the start of routes and, although they can hardly be recommended, might be used on the route at a pinch. There is also a 1:250 000 map (Holiday Map, sheet 4), which is useful for overall planning.

LONG DISTANCE WAYS

The Beara Way, which mostly follows abandoned roads and tracks, circles the Beara peninsula and is about 200km long. Though it reaches 300m high in a few places it is generally routed much lower. The Beara Way has several sub-loops. A map/guide to the Way has been published by Cork Kerry Tourism.

The 85km-long Sheep's Head Way travels round the peninsula south of Beara. It runs partly inland, partly along the spine and partly along the coast of the peninsula. There is an excellent guide to the Way.

Remember that, as stated above, the Ways are badly depicted on the OS maps.

A FEW ROUTE SELECTIONS

The following selection gives a variety of routes and might be worth considering if you want to get an idea (no more than that!) of what the area has to offer.

- Route 5 or 6: Memorable, rocky circuits around deep-set valleys in North Beara, with route 6 much the more strenuous.
- Routes 10, 15 or 17: Routes to Hungry Hill and Sugarloaf, taking in mighty cliffs and slabs in magnificent scenery.
- Route 26 or 29: Two highly scenic areas of west Cork, the former little frequented and the latter well-known, though both offer rugged and rewarding terrain. Route 26 is preferable if you have to choose.
- Routes 11 or 25: Varied sea-cliff scenery in the Beara and Sheep's Head peninsulas respectively, both areas suitable for leisurely pottering.

SAFETY

Walkers unused to Irish (and British) conditions will be excused if they are asked to read carefully a section on safety, given that the highest mountain in the entire region is a puny 706m.

Do not be misled by such seemingly insignificant heights! Irish mountains in general (and this region is no exception) are wild, remote and worthy of respect. It is noteworthy that a high proportion of the fatal accidents in recent years has been suffered by visitors who did not realise the conditions they were to face.

But let's not be too timid. If you take reasonable precautions and do not try walking in conditions for which you are unprepared, you will enjoy your time in the mountains and return to base safely and with a sense of having achieved something worthwhile.

So, what are reasonable precautions?

- You will get some idea of what to expect on each route from the section on 'Difficulties'. Of course, conditions vary greatly depending on the weather but you can assume that unless the route is entirely or almost entirely on road, track or path you should wear walking boots.
- The section on 'Difficulties' will also give you an idea of how hard it will be to find your way round the route, but remember that the easiest route to follow in bad visibility may be harder than the hardest in good. Cloud and fog make all the difference to navigation. As well as the obvious lack of visibility they are disorienting and distorting, so that what is in reality a minor hill near at hand will appear through cloud like a major mountain much further away.
- It is definitely prudent not to walk alone and better to have at least four persons. This allows one to stay with the victim if there is an accident and two to try to get help. If the worst comes to the worst, you can summon the mountain rescue by phoning 112 or 999.
- Leave word at base of where you intend to go and what time you intend to be back.
- Get a weather forecast before you go.

WHAT TO CARRY WITH YOU

If you were to carry all the equipment that some experts advise you to carry, you would be so weighed down that you wouldn't be able to walk.

The most important item to get right are boots, as mentioned above. Apart from that there are only a few things that you really must carry. These include food and a flask with a hot liquid, and a map and compass. Map and compass are no good unless you know how to use them! Unless the day looks uncommonly settled and likely to remain so, you should take a waterproof. Lastly, you need a rucksack to put everything else in. Anything else is optional or depends mainly on the weather and the route.

RIGHTS OF WAY AND GOOD CONDUCT

Nearly all the land over which you walk in this region, the major exceptions being the waymarked paths, belongs to someone and *you are his or her uninvited guest*. Landowners are generally trusting folk and will not object to your walking across their land. Do not abuse the privilege - and that is what it is. Remember this and behave accordingly. Specifically:

- Respect the privacy of the occupants of houses. If you have to walk through a farmyard, ask permission and do so quietly.
- Do not bring dogs into sheep rearing country, that is nearly everywhere in the mountains.
- Do not stand on fence wire. It may look the same afterwards but will have been irretrievably damaged. If you have to cross stone walls, do not dislodge stones.
- Leave gates just as you found them. Climb them at the hinged end.
- Do not litter the mountains - or anywhere else for that matter. You would be doing a singular service to other hill walkers if you would remove some litter that you find in remote areas such as mountain summits.

THEY'RE YOUR MOUNTAINS TOO - GET INVOLVED!

I wish I could say that the beauty of Ireland's mountains was reflected in the care and attention that we, the Irish people, pay to our environment. Alas, it isn't. There is no need to elaborate, except to state that because I have usually not mentioned specific instances of littering and dumping in these pages does not mean that I have not noticed them or have not been saddened by them. South Kerry and west Cork, by the way, seems to be no worse than most areas in Ireland and a lot better than some.

Would that there were a simple solution to this problem, which is caused both by an ingrained couldn't-care-less attitude on the part of too many people and an unwillingness on the part of the responsible authorities to enforce laws. All I can suggest here is that you get involved in any organisation that tries to look after the environment and that if you are in a walking club that you ensure that there is an active conservation group and get involved in it.

USEFUL CONTACTS

Irish Bus/Bus Eireann, Capwell Cork. ☎ 021-506066.

Irish Rail Cork. ☎ 021- 504888.

Independent Holiday Hostels, 57 Lr Gardiner St, Dublin 1. ☎ 01-836 4700.

South West Regional Tourism Organisation, Monument Buildings, Grand Parade, Cork. ☎ 021- 273251.

Irish Youth Hostel Association / An Oige, 61 Mountjoy Street, Dublin 7. ☎ 01-830 4555.

Mountaineering Council of Ireland, House of Sport, Longmile Road, Dublin 12. ☎ 01-450 9845.

NORTH BEARA

This area covers roughly the part of the Beara Peninsula that is in county Kerry and is west of the N71.

This is undoubtedly the most demanding - and probably the most rewarding - area covered by this book. Running south from the shores of the Kenmare River (it's not a river, more a wide inlet) are a series of delectable valleys, six of which are explored in these pages. The summits themselves are generally not distinguished, and rarely rise in classical cones. However their flanks, falling in more than a few places in cliffs and great bands of slab, are most impressive. The best-known of all these high-level circuits of valleys is at Cummeengeera (route 5). Baurearagh (route 4) and Glenbeg (route 6) are similar to it but not so demanding, while Glanrastel, Glantrasna and to some extent Glaninchiquin and Barraduff (routes 3, 7-9 respectively) all take in part of the valley floor as well as the heights. The shorter walks cover the lovely wooded area around Lauragh (route 2) and a low-level exploration of a remote valley (route 1) . All in all, an area of great character and diversity.

ROUTE 1: CUMMEENGEERA VALLEY

A walk into the inner recesses of one of the loneliest and most dramatic parts of the whole peninsula. With some rocky and boggy terrain, this is not quite as easy as its short distance and climb might indicate. You can also walk most of the Cummeengeera circuit (route 5) from the end of this route.

Getting There: As in route 5, except that you drive onward from its starting point and park at the end of tarmac near a farmhouse (GR 754553). **Bus** 282.

Walking Time: 1.75 hours (distance 4km, climb 100m), including 0.5 hours over Naismith for generally difficult terrain. However you will probably want to wander round the upper valley so give yourself lots more time.

Difficulties: Some rocky ground underfoot. Easy navigationally.

Map: None necessary but take sheet 84 if you have it. The sketch map for this route is on page 18.

Route: Take the rough road, which later becomes a track, onward from the parking place. It crosses the Drimminboy River, the main stream in the valley, before fading away. Then climb steeply on its extension as an intermittent path, keeping crags up on the right, into the high and almost flat upper valley. At the end of it you will see the remains of a village on the right under a huge expanse of sandstone slab. An awesome spot.

Return by the same route. Alternatively, for a little more adventure, you can walk downstream with the river on the right, climb over high ground which plunges into the river and beyond it descend on a track which ends on tarmac.■

ROUTE 2: KNOCKANOUGHANISH AND KNOCKATEE

If you want a (fairly) painless introduction to the terrain and views of the Beara Peninsula you could do worse than take this short walk near Lauragh. Some rocks and slabs, some boggy ground, a section of the Beara Way and lots of varied scenery considering the modest heights (386m, 330m) attained.

Getting There: Park in the village of Lauragh (GR 7758), let's say opposite the church for the purposes of description. **Bus 282.**

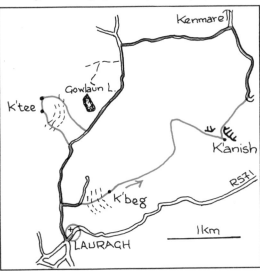

Walking Time: 4 hours (distance 12km, climb 680m), which is a little faster than Naismith given that much of the terrain is on track or road, though there are also two steep descents. This time may be shortened to 3.25 hours (distance 10km, climb 500m) by omitting Knockatee, though if you have the time do not miss it.

Difficulties: None.

Map: Sheet 84.

Route: From the church walk downhill to the nearby cross-roads and turn right, so following the Beara Way. This takes you through nicely wooded country, which unfortunately doesn't last long. Turn first right onto a track and about where the track swings at right-angles left leave it to climb through slabs to Knockbeg (172m).

From the summit head roughly north-east, keeping to high - and wet - ground and to the right of upland fields (they spoil the illusion that you are in a remote area) aiming for the end of the long westward-running spur of Knockanoughanish. Once on it the terrain is drier, but instead fences form a hazard. Several will have to be climbed, but do so carefully. The target here is of course Knockanoughanish (386m), reached by a short but stiff climb over easy terrain. The twin-peaked summit offers predictably good views with Glanrastel (route 9) off to the south-east and Cummeengeera to the south-west (route 5).

From Knockanoughanish some care is needed. Walk north-east down a steep but negotiable rocky spur and as you approach the road (R571) look out for a point to reach it without crossing more fences than you have to. On the road turn left and walk for about 1km. This is what passes for a main road in these tranquil parts, but in spite of the modest burden of traffic it carries you might be happier when you turn left onto a narrow road that is part of the Beara Way.

From this junction walk about 1.5km to a tee and turn left here. You can walk all the way directly back to Lauragh from here - it's a long incline, all on road (just about describable as road anyway) into remote country and then an equally long descent into Lauragh. Alternatively, it is well worthwhile climbing Knockatee for the unsurpassed views it gives of Kilmakilloge Harbour and the entire area round the Kenmare River. To climb it take the Beara Way road until you are past Gowlaun Lough and the fields around it. Then turn right off the road to climb, initially avoiding gorse and then the worst of the slabs, so as to reach the lower northern summit. From there climb the short distance to the main summit, crowned by a high rectangular cairn. Descend south-east from the summit to the crest of the road and walk into Lauragh.■

ROUTE 3: BARRADUFF

A wide valley, fields and scattered woods on its floor, is bordered on two sides by wide, flat spurs and on the third by more rugged, slabby country. The circuit of this valley along these spurs makes for not the most attractive of walks but, apart from excellent long-distance views it has two pluses: it can easily be shortened, and if you have no transport it is possible to walk all the (Beara) Way from Kenmare.

Getting There: Cross the bridge south in Kenmare, taking the R571 road for over 2½ miles (4km). Here turn left signposted Dawros Church. At the Church turn left and right at the nearby crossroads. Drive for over another mile to a fork and park on the waste ground here (GR 889664). You can also walk from Kenmare or get the 282 bus.

Walking Time: 4.5 hours (distance 13km, climb 720m), though as said above this may easily be greatly shortened.

Difficulties: One rough, steep descent. In indistinct country, which much of this route crosses, some care is needed in navigation.

Map: Sheet 85. The Beara Way is very badly depicted.

Route: Take the right fork (south-west) of the Beara Way along a narrow road, shortly branching off it (the road) to follow the Way on a path to the right of a farmhouse. Since the Beara Way is to be followed roughly south-west right to the crest of the hill ahead, detailed directions are probably unnecessary, even though the Way, over gently sloping moorland, is none too clearly waymarked and in bad conditions especially, a modicum of compass work may be needed.

This crest is where you must leave the dubious life-line of the Way. Before setting off along the top of the broad ridge to the south-east, it is certainly worthwhile looking over the crest of the ridge to the west where mountains and cliffs dominate the lakes on the floor of Glaninchiquin. After that climb through soggy ground to pt 410m and continue along the broad ridge, keeping the cliffs over Cummer Lough off to the left. This course will take you past a great V cut in the cliffs south of Cummer Lough, a modest reassurance point in moderately bad weather, and since you won't recognise it in really bad weather no use at all when you really need it.

Point 484m is the next target. It gives excellent views in all directions (the great slabs encountered in route 4 should be prominent to the south-west) though it has a far from distinct summit. Do not despair of navigation however: just to its east is a dense block of forest reaching from the south right to the crest of the hill and since it is the only forest for miles around it is an unmistakable reassurance point.

Which is just as well, as the leg from this forest, the steep descent to the road carrying the Beara Way should be carefully negotiated. You will see two north-east running spurs on the map, but both have rough ground and occasional crags so the best plan is to descend through the valley between them, following a stream and so reaching the narrow road just to the west of its highest point.

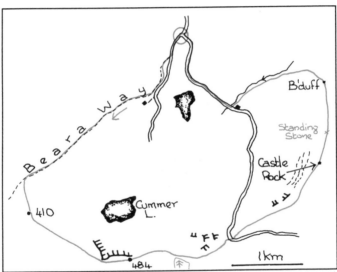

Turn right onto the road and walk a few metres uphill to the crest where there is a rough path on the left heading towards Castle Rock (395m). A ridge develops on this ascent, and the slabs underfoot make for easy going, while the cliffs cut into the western side of Castle Rock's summit promise dramatic terrain later on.

Alas, the descent north from Castle Rock offers nothing more interesting near at hand than a sizeable standing stone, set in a broad boggy ridge (yes, another one). From the stone climb shapeless Barraduff (400m) and then swing north-west off the summit ridge to pick up a stream running south-west. Follow this down to a track visible well before you reach it. This track ends directly above a house, which you should keep on the left in order to reach tarmac. Turn right for the start, which is over 1km away along a narrow pleasant road. ■

ROUTE 4: THE BAUREARAGH CIRCUIT

A steep but short climb onto a broad ridge overlooking hill and coastal scenery centred on the lovely lakes of Glaninchiquin is followed by a steeper but shorter climb over broad, smooth slabs to a soft and grassy plateau. Beyond this is an easy and scenic stroll along a high and in places, narrow ridge. In all a memorable and rewarding circuit.

Getting There: From Glengarriff take the N71 for about 9 miles (14km), here cross the bridge over the Baurearagh River (signposted), take the nearby next turn left into Baurearagh and drive for a further 3.2 miles (5.1km) to a track on the right and another a few metres further on the left (GR 879616). There is limited room for parking here, so you may have to seek parking on the margins along the track to the left. Park considerately. This point may also be reached from Kenmare. You can see the sign for the Baurearagh River before you make the turn right into Baurearagh.

Walking Time: 4.5 hours (distance 11km, climb 670m), including about 15 minutes over Naismith to allow for steep descents.

Difficulties: Some moderately difficult navigation near the start but otherwise quite easy. The ground is generally good underfoot, though the steep descents, especially that at the end, will probably prove tiring.

Map: Sheet 85.

Route: From the car you can see almost the entire circuit reaching around the valley and back the other side in hairpin fashion. I hope (and am fairly sure) that you will find that it looks interesting.

Take the track on the right (north), leave it when it shortly swings right and continue upward through a field, keeping the farmhouse well on the right to avoid disturbing the residents. Beyond it, and now in rough country, climb directly upward so greatly extending an already wide view. When you reach an earthbank some way up the hill, you can start climbing diagonally left, thus veering away from Knocknagorraveela (507m), a dumpy, characterless mountain, and so hardly worth climbing. You will therefore reach a boggy plateau to its south, not interesting in itself but giving marvellous views down towards the loughs of Glaninchiquin and later to the highly impressive corrie gouged into the north-east shoulder of Coomnadiha.

As you walk roughly south across this plateau you will see a small, rocky peak ahead and beyond it ... what's this? ... a seemingly almost vertical slab of rock directly on the route. Yes, you do have to climb it, but be assured that, in spite of appearances, it is not steep. The small rocky peak makes for a delightful climb, its character enhanced by a small lake sheltering into its right flank. Make the short descent from this peak to a low point directly facing the rock slabs. This point is easily identifiable and marks a good escape route; you can descend from here on a grassy gully running initially at 60°. A descent is certainly possible from further along the circuit, but from points which are difficult to identify.

Climb the slabs, where you will find that only when you have to transfer from one to another is there any difficulty. At the top you are into very different and duller country: a little boggy underfoot, though the views remain marvellous.

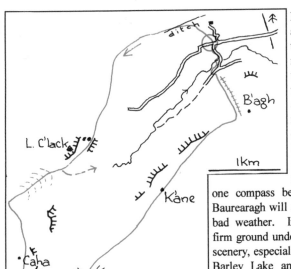

From here on the cliffs and steep ground on the left are a good navigational aid. You will first climb south to drear Caha (608m), an undistinguished mound, and then push on north-east towards Baurearagh which is about 4km away. Once you face north-east one compass bearing all the way to Baurearagh will almost suffice, even in bad weather. In good weather, with firm ground underfoot and some lovely scenery, especially towards the sizeable Barley Lake and the indented coast around Glengarriff, you will be able to enjoy the walk to the full.

Before you reach Baurearagh you will probably encounter a lake about 20m long on the summit of Killane (537m). After it you should watch out for a fence on the near side of Baurearagh (489m), an undistinguished peak that is hardly worth climbing. Turn left at the fence (I hope fencing hasn't been augmented by the time you are there, as it will confuse matters) and follow it all the way down.

Close to the road there is fencing and a low band of cliff At the time of writing (late 1998) the easiest way to evade both is to walk to the left, but new fencing may soon make it easier to walk to the right. When you reach the road, however you manage it, turn right and then left over the bridge to reach the car. ■

ROUTE 5: THE CUMMEENGEERA CIRCUIT

A dramatic terrain of highly contorted rock strata makes for hard going to start, after which is a high-level walk along the edge of cliffs and steep slopes with magnificent views down into the head of the remote valley of Cummeengeera.

Getting There: The start is about 17 miles (27km) south-west of Kenmare. Take the R571 to Lauragh (GR 7758). Still on the R571, continue straight ahead through the scattered village, turning left at the sign 'Glanmore Lake'. Take the first right after 0.6 miles and park after another 0.9 miles around the junction on the left (GR 763560). Parking is hard to find on the narrow road and you may have to search around if your party has more than 2 or 3 cars. **Bus** 282.

Walking Time: 6 hours (distance 12km, climb 1080m) including 0.75 hours over Naismith for route finding and difficult terrain near the start and 15 minutes for a fairly steep descent near the end.

Difficulties: Some slabs to negotiate at the start; otherwise the terrain is fairly good. Navigation is quite easy in good weather except for the section between the first summit, Cummeenahillan, and the trig pillar on Coomacloghane. This section is quite serious even in good visibility and likely to be a nightmare of indistinct 'summits' in bad. The variation below avoids this section. Be wary about attempting an escape route in the first half of the route as there are extensive sections of difficult slabs close to the valley floor that not marked on the map. If you can, keep going to make an easy descent after Bireca.

Map: Sheet 84.

Route: From the junction on the left around which you parked, walk back the way you came to the first bungalow, now on the left. Just beyond it take the gated driveway uphill, cross another gate and just before the first and only farmhouse on this driveway turn left into open country.

The first task is to climb Cummeennahillan. Here the problem, apart from evading gorse and ferns, is to avoid being driven leftward by the lie of the rock strata, so that in order to keep on course your route will be along a series of easy grassy ramps followed by the difficult crossing of rocky slabs on the right. Cummeenahillan (356m) is a magnificent viewpoint, particularly of the highly contorted strata of the route ahead. It has no definite summit marker but the boggy plain just to its west is sufficient retrospective evidence that you have climbed it.

The next target is Knocknaveachal. As indicated above this is difficult area navigationally, with rocky outcrops, slabs and grassy ramps. There are two notional summits both of 513m, with a distinct swing from west to south-west to get from one to the other. Not that the approach to the next mountain, Tooth is much better. There is an easily avoidable, long, almost vertical slab on the way to Tooth, or at least there is on some approaches so don't be surprised if you don't find it. The summit (590m) is marked by a jumble of puddles and rocky outcrops and so is almost impossible to identify exactly. However, after it the terrain is much easier, with outcrops and much soft ground and this transition may be some help in extremis.

Coomacloghane (599m), the next mountain to be climbed, is more accommodating. Though this 'peak' barely rises above the surrounding bogland, it does have a trig pillar, an unmistakable landmark. From Coomacloghane walk south-west for over a kilometre to reach the grassy plateau marking the high ground on the south-west side of Cummeengeera.

Having attained this plateau at Motidhu (584m) the rule is to keep cliffs and steep ground on the left, walking south-east at first and then swinging left to take in the undistinguished Eskatarriff (over 640m) and then the small but steep-sided rocky pinnacle of Bireca (531m), an excellent landmark. From about here onward the views down into Cummeengeera are nothing short of magnificent, considerably better than those from the opposite side of the valley. You should easily be able to see the tiny deserted village down in the valley, sheltering under stern slabs and cliffs. At the low point just beyond Bireca it is easy to escape down into the valley, though considering the walk ahead, I hope this isn't necessary.

Continuing along the high ground beyond this escape point there is a short but stiff climb to Lackabane (605m) and hardly any climb to its sister peak, Curraghreague (over 590m), which has high cliffs on its north-west side that drop in long columns into the glen far below. This may be a useful reassurance point since the descent is nigh.

But not that nigh. The route runs north-east from Curraghreague to a col from which it looks as if there is an easy descent to the start. Not so. This direct approach is an area of hidden rocks and high vegetation so it is necessary to climb about 30m to the next hill, pt 406m. From here descend north to a level grassy area and then make what will probably prove to be a tedious descent to a prominent ringfort visible from a distance. At the ringfort take a path northwards, which shortly becomes a narrow track, and then a wider track. Cross the Drimminboy River on it to reach the nearby start.

'Easier' Variation: Easier in the sense that this route avoids the navigationally difficult terrain at the start of the main route. However, it does include some hard clambering over rocks along a semi-waterfall, which might not be everybody's idea of fun. *Do not attempt this variation in the reverse direction.*

Take route 1 to the most remote ruin in the deserted village and climb by the stream in the gully directly behind the house. If it's any consolation the first part of this climb is the hardest. When you emerge onto comparatively level ground, you can turn right to cross another gully and then walk across easy ground to Loughanunaghan (a lake) to the north-west. From here walk either to the col to the west or, if you require further assurance, to the trig pillar on Coomacloghane. You can pick up the main route from either point. ■

ROUTE 6: CIRCUIT OF GLENBEG

Inland of Ardgroom lies Glenbeg Lough, stern lines of steep ground overlooking the sides of its valley and the impressive haystack of Skellig guarding its entrance. The walk ascends steeply into rugged country overlooking the deep valley of Cummeengeera, descends sharply to a lovely viewpoint at the head of the lake and traverses the high ground on its south. A varied and scenic walk.

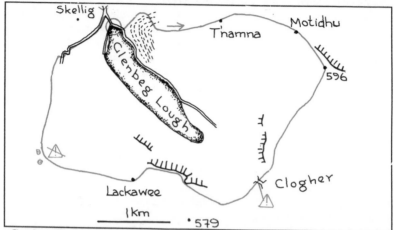

Getting There: Turn south in Ardgroom (21 miles (34km) from Kenmare) at the sign for Glenbeg and park in the carpark at the lake (GR 702538). **Bus 282.**

Walking Time: 4.75 hours (distance 11km, climb 920m).

Difficulties: Careful navigation required especially in the centre section where there are few landmarks. Some rocky and boggy terrain but mostly good underfoot.

Map: Sheet 84.

Route: With the great lines of crags on Tooreennamna, the first peak to be climbed, rising steeply close at hand, a direct ascent might display a little too much bravado. So walk about 100m onward from the carpark, turn left off the road here and climb upward along a narrow gully, with the crags rising close above on the right.

You will have to judge for yourself when you can turn right from the gully and start a direct climb to the summit ridge: the longer you avoid it the further you will have to walk. However, having gained the ridge and easier ground you can enjoy excellent views in all directions and an exhilaratingly narrow rocky stretch on the way to the far from exhilarating almost flat summit (over 520m).

From here on there are few clear navigational landmarks; indeed the trig pillar on Coomacloghane (GR 7354) is the best indicator of your position, though of course it won't be visible in bad weather when you most need it. With this gloomy thought in mind head directly east to Motidhu (pt 584m), initially following an indistinct ditch from Tooreennamna.

Motidhu itself, set in a region of peat-hags is quite difficult to identify. The only real clue to indicate that you have overshot it is the steep ground you then face overlooking Cummeengeera far below. Swing south-east from the notional summit (or that steep ground) to reach Eskatarriff (pt 596m) only 500m away, all of it boggy ground.

From Eskatarriff swing south downhill aiming for a low point at the head of Glenbeg Lough, which in spite of its modest height (300m) gives excellent views along the lake and in the opposite direction into the lonely, flat valley of Clogher, flat that is, except where broken by occasional rocky outcrops, islands in a calm sea (route 10).

At 2.5 hours into the walk you can retreat from this low point to the valley floor, but since further treats lie in store, I hope you won't. Climb south-west from here towards pt 579m, initially over steep, rocky ground. There is little point in climbing to this summit; instead walk beside developing cliffs on the right until you reach the cliff's highest point just east of Lackawee (572m), and then climb to its boggy summit.

From Lackawee head west along a wide, undulating ridge, crossing over a fence on the right when opportune to avoid a high cross-ways fence later on near two small lakes. Beyond these lakes veer right off the crest of the ridge so aiming for rocky Skellig and later for the highest two houses on the road below. At the time of writing it is possible to gain the road between these houses without crossing a fence, but you may have to judge it for yourself when you get there. However you manage it - and whatever you do, do not damage fences - turn left downhill onto the road and walk less than 1km to the carpark. ■

ROUTE 7: GLANINCHIQUIN

The focus of a long valley sheltering a series of large and scenic lakes is at its far end where a high waterfall is set amidst steep and rugged slopes, some of them clothed by mixed woods. This route approaches the end of the valley by a gently rising but not over-exciting ridge and then descends through rugged terrain from behind the waterfall to the valley floor.

Getting There: Take the R571 from Kenmare, branching left after 8 miles (13km) at the sign for Glaninchiquin. Drive for a further 2.1 miles (3.4km) to park at the track on the right, which is on the Beara Way. This point may also be easily reached on the R571 from the west. **Bus** 282.

Walking Time: 5.5 hours (distance 14km, climb 820m) including about 15 minutes over Naismith for the steep descent to Lough Coominlack.

Difficulties: Some rough terrain and a little navigation that requires attention, but nothing too serious. You may be asked for money to cross the land at the far end of Glaninchiquin. Since you are just using some of the amenities provided only because there is no alternative, it would seem unfair to be asked to pay. However it might be prudent to carry a few pounds extra, just in case (or alternatively, to carry no money at all, so that you are impervious to pleas).

Map: Both sheets 84 and 85. The transition from one to the other is not too difficult. Note that waterfalls (two are encountered on this route) are not precisely indicated on the OS maps but are on the sketch map given here.

Route: Take the Beara Way track south-west between two of the large lakes in the valley, Upper Cloonee Lough and Lough Inchiquin. Beyond them, and still on the Way, climb gently through a mixed woodland. Walk a few hundred metres beyond the first house and here leave the Way to start the climb through awkward slabs towards the first peak, Knockagarrane (414m). Just to its south-east drop steeply to a tiny lake set in a gorge. From here on for some distance the route, steadily upward south-east along the broad ridge, is over soft ground where you can make good progress. This terrain is a far cry from the ground overlooking Lough Napeasta down on the left: here the slabs rising from the shore look like a steeply rising ploughed field (see the sketch on page 55).

Knockreagh (500m) is the next target. Rather than trying to find this peak

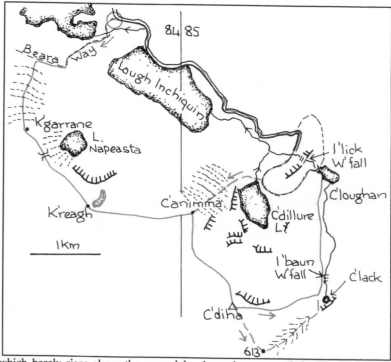

which barely rises above the general level you have a much better chance of finding Lough Naneeslee, a moderately large lake and a good setting for a break. From here take the distinct drop to the east of Knockreagh after which, and here you cross over onto sheet 85, you should swing slightly left to take in Cummeenanimma (over 480m). Cummeenanimma is similar to Knockreagh in that its summit is indistinct. Otherwise it is quite different since it offers magnificent views over the end of Glaninchiquin, which is, as mentioned in the introduction to this route, a region to savour.

The next target is Coomnadiha. To get there walk initially south from Cummeenanimma, passing round one magnificent corrie on the left overlooking

Cummeenadillure Lough and partly passing round another. The trig pillar on Coomnadiha (644m, 3.25 hours) is a useful landmark, as it is reassuring to be sure of your starting point for the next stretch, ending at Lough Coominlack to the east, which is a little tricky navigationally. However before you set off you might note that if you have not walked route 4 and do not intend to do so, this might be a good opportunity to descend the slabs climbed in that route; it's a more scenic descent to Lough Coominlack than that given here. See below.

For the main route walk east from the trig pillar, so traversing the edge of the second corrie you met on the way up. Then descend on one of several rocky spurs reaching east to the small valley west of Lough Coominlack. On this descent you should see the great slabs mentioned in route 4 off to the right, just one item in what is by any standards spectacular scenery.

The near side of Lough Coominlack is pretty wet, and since the idea now is to follow its outlet stream you don't have to venture to its shore. The outlet stream plunges over low and modest Ishaghbaun Waterfall shortly after leaving the lake; it is not difficult to find a way down roughly parallel to it.

Below the stream you have a choice: you can keep to the stream, so walking through a tussocky and fairly wet plain all the way down to Cummeenaloughan (it's a lake) over 1km away or you can keep above the plain by walking along the higher ground to its left. If you keep to the stream you can walk on either bank since there is a bridge on the north end of Cummeenaloughan. However, no matter what you do the other bank will appear to be better underfoot!

At Cummeenaloughan you are into 'scenic development' territory. Specifically whether you want it or not you are provided with paths, tracks and picnic tables. Take the path running south-west from the bridge at the outlet stream (if you have kept to the higher ground, simply turn left when you meet it). This will take you over a shoulder and then down to Cummeenadillure Lough, the selfsame lake you saw earlier from the Cummeenanimma area. You now have a chance to admire it from a very different angle, and set in a deep bowl with cliffs and high ground in all directions except north, it certainly is impressive.

At Cummeenadillure Lough a track starts (or rather ends). Follow it close to the foot of Ishaghbuderlick Waterfall and from there onto a gradually improving road. It's nearly 4km back to the start, all on road, but a particularly scenic one, so the plodding time shouldn't feel too long.

Variation on the Descent from Coomnadiha: As mentioned above a more spectacular descent. From the trig pillar walk 800m south-east to pt 613m (it should take about 10 minutes). Then descend north-east on slabs to Lough Coominlack and pick up the main route from here.

Short Variation: Park in the amenity area carpark at the head of the valley (GR 856623), where you will have to pay the entrance fee. Take the track to Cummeenadillure Lough and climb Cummeenanimma from here (you will see an easy, grassy line on the left of the crest of the spur). Follow the main route from here. When you get back to Cummeenaloughan you may like to follow the path north from the bridge to vary the outward walk. Walking time is 3.75 hours (distance 9km, climb 640m). ∎

ROUTE 8: GLANTRASNA

A steep initial climb out of Glantrasna into boggy country bordered by impressive cliffs is followed by a walk via a scenic upland lake into the short, narrow, enclosed valley of Glantrasna. A somewhat easier and less dramatic version of route 9.

Getting There: From Kenmare take the R751 for about 9 miles (14km) to pass the sign for Tuosist on the right. The road then climbs steeply and as it descends again towards Laragh watch out for a shrine on the right and a side road running acutely back directly opposite it. Take this side road for 1.8 miles (2.9km) to park near the bridge - there is room for several cars (GR 826597). It's easier to

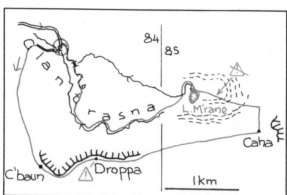

find the side road from the Lauragh direction. **Bus** 282.

Walking Time: 4 hours (distance 10km, climb 700m) including a little time over Naismith for one steep descent back into Glantrasna.

Difficulties: The mid-section of this route has quite a lot of featureless terrain and care is needed in bad visibility. In spite of much boggy country the underfoot conditions are generally satisfactory. The steep descent has already been mentioned.

Map: Alas, both sheets 84 and 85 are required and the transition from one to the other (and back again) is none too easy.

Route: Cross the concrete bridge and walk up the road beyond. At any point around the nearby last house leave the road and head upwards, keeping to the crest of the slope to increase the range of views westward. There are some rocky outcrops between the boggy areas on the way to Derreenataggart (304m), the first 'peak' and something of a non-event. This terrain continues to Cummeenbaun (510m), where views open out over Glanrastel and the great cliffs beyond it. Indeed from here on you are not short of cliffs near at hand: as you walk onward to Droppa (522m), there are most impressive cliffs visible back towards Cummeenbaun and directly north of Droppa itself.

From Droppa head directly (a compass bearing of about 90° will take you over the border of sheet 84 onto 85) towards Caha over fairly soft ground, initially with cliffs still on the left. Along here, in good visibility anyway, the trig pillar on Coomnadiha gives a good indication of your position. The summit of Caha (608m) is merely a slight rise in a boggy plateau. However if you venture just a little further east you will have an excellent view over steep ground into the valley of the Baurearagh River (route 4). Caha - or rather this steep ground to its east - offers another advantage: the sudden increase in slope is a definite clue to your position in otherwise featureless terrain.

From Caha walk north to the comparatively low ground only a few hundred metres away and then descend west into the valley containing Lough Macournane, where there is easy ground underfoot but more than occasional slabs and crags on the higher hillside on both sides.

If nowhere else is, Lough Macourane is certainly unmistakable. A large lake set in rugged surroundings, it makes an excellent setting for a rest. After which, onward. Start by following the outlet stream first north-west, then south and then south-west, all in a few hundred metres. However when it swings away west continue onward and (for a short distance) upward towards the south-west, picking up a stream as you finally start on a steep downhill. At the start of this downhill you are back onto sheet 84 (at about GR 840587) at the head of Glantrasna.

So, all you have to do now is follow the stream downhill to the start? Well, not quite. It certainly is a lovely, easy walk along the valley floor with excellent views up to the cliffs on the south along whose tops you walked earlier, but your troubles are not quite over. After about 1km along the stream (keep it on the left) you will round a corner and see fields along the valley sides ahead. With varied but mostly uninviting terrain looming perhaps the best bet here is to keep these fields on the left and follow whatever snatch of track or path you encounter until you reach the first house, a deserted one. Here you can pick up a track that leads across a concrete bridge and onward to the similar concrete bridge at which you parked, only a few hundred metres on. ■

ROUTE 9: GLANRASTEL

A lovely long walk along the serpentine writhings of Glanrastel, a valley all of 6km long with a wealth of varied views. After it, a steady climb to Cushaficulla (594m) and Knockowen (658m), whose cliffs overlook Glanrastal, and a rocky descent back to the valley.

Getting There: From Lauragh (GR 7758), about 14 miles (22km) west of Kenmare, take the R574 (Healy Pass Road), turning first left off it after An Sibin pub. Drive for 1.5 miles (2.4km) on a narrow road, at which point you will see a right turn climbing steeply. Don't take it: instead continue for another few hundred metres to park at an open space that will take several cars (GR 804582). **Bus** 282.

This point is equally easily reached from Healy Pass, the right turn into Glanrastel being the only one for miles.

Walking Time: 4.25 hours (distance 10km, climb 700m) including about 15 minutes over Naismith for the difficult descent at the end.

Difficulties: A tough descent over slabs at the end of the walk. Otherwise fairly easy terrain and no more than moderately difficult navigation.

Map: Sheet 84, but since you are going to be alarmingly close to the border with sheet 85 take it also if you have it.

Route: Take the southward-bound track of the several going every which way at the start and you will soon find yourself at the entrance to the valley. It might be no bad idea to study carefully the ground to the right, as you enter the valley and see if you can find a better way down than described here. What with clumps of rhododendron, hidden rocks and high vegetation I found it quite a battle to gain the road just north of the last house in the valley. But more of that anon.

Once you get into the valley simply walk along its length, following a deteriorating track so that you are eventually walking on rough ground parallel to the river. As you advance you will pass under the great contorted line of cliffs

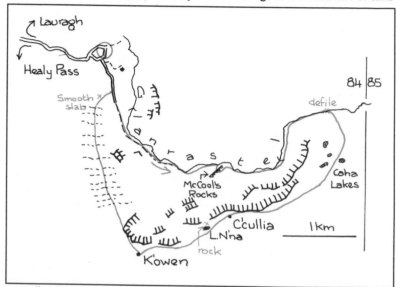

guarding Knockowen and later you will have to negotiate the slabs called Finn McCool's rocks (veer right from the river to climb them). Beyond the rocks, and here the valley has swung north, you will see ahead a rocky line of rising ground on the right of the valley floor. Having passed it, and here the valley swings east, you enter a narrow defile. At about this point leave the valley floor and head to Caha lakes to the south. The shore of one of these lakes makes a good place for a rest and a bite to eat.

Keeping cliffs on the right climb Cushnaficulla (594m), a twin-peaked summit with a minor gorge between the summits and beyond it descend to Lough Namuinna, on whose shore is a rock with a remarkable square cross-section.

West of Lough Namuinna climb to Knockowen (658m). Its northern side is truncated by a great curve of corrie towering above Glanrastel - you will already have noticed this feature from below. The second-highest peak on the peninsula, it commands excellent views to the plateau of Hungry Hill to the south-west, Sugarloaf to the south-east and the of mountains on Iveragh to the north.

Keeping the cliffs on the right climb the northern top (over 560m) and then continue initially north-west into a difficult terrain of slabs, each requiring a detour or a short but awkward direct descent. (If you want to avoid all this keep well over to the left where the terrain is easier but duller.) As you advance swing gradually north to keep to the crest of the spur.

The problem now (obviously) is to reach the track in Glanrastel on which you started. If you haven't any other ideas walk (or stumble, since the terrain is difficult) to a huge, smooth rock slab partly facing towards the valley floor and located close to the last houses, and then walk directly to the nearby track. Lick your wounds, and turn left for the nearby start.

Short Variation: There is little climbing and the prospect of great cliff scenery if you attempt only the valley section of this walk. You can walk as far as you like and as long as you follow the (or even *a*) stream you can't go wrong! I suggest you turn back at the defile where those on the main route leave the valley floor. Walking time is 2.25 hours (distance 9km, climb 150m). ■

ROUTE 10: HUNGRY HILL FROM THE NORTH

An exciting and challenging climb from the end of the deep valley of Glanmore to lofty Hungry Hill (685m) and then over rocky terrain into a remote upland valley. The walk ends with a steep descent by the side of rapids back down into Glanmore. Definitely not a walk for the inexperienced or even the experienced on a bad day.

Getting There: From Laragh (GR 7758) follow the signs for the youth hostel, and park about 2 miles beyond it at a left turn (GR 757524). (You may take this left turn and drive about a half-mile further where there is limited parking, thus eliminating a road walk at each end, but the road is very narrow and bumpy and the walk attractive, so it can hardly be recommended.)

Walking Time: 5.5 hours (distance 13km, climb 760m), thus allowing about 15 minutes over Naismith for each of: route finding on the initial ascent, negotiating slabs on the final climb to Hungry Hill and a steep descent at the end.

Difficulties: Steep (if not hazardous) climbing to start and some difficult navigation. And don't forget that this is remote territory with little hope of help if you get into difficulties.

Map: Sheet 84. The map gives little indication of the relative magnitudes of the various watercourses at the start of the route so you may find the accompanying commentary (below) some use.

Route: Before starting it might be useful to give an overview of this, the end of Glanmore. The road down which you drove faced the small northern sub-valley, which has one gorge falling into it. This sub-valley is separated from the main valley by the low but formidable Esknamaggy, a spur with an alligator-like spine and more recommended for scrambling than walking.

Starting at the right, the main valley has a wide cascade and a small tributary gorge, both just above a small wood; a straight narrow gorge which unaccountably is the one indicated as the major watercourse on sheet 84 and a few streams (the number depend on exactly what you count), which here and there steepen into waterfalls, on the face of the valley facing north-west. You won't, of course, see all these from the one spot but you might note that the route ascends by the last mentioned streams and descends by the wide cascade.

Walk the side road round the nose of Esknamaggy and thence into the main valley. At the bridge about 1km from the start you should have a look at the area of the streams where you are going to ascend. What follows is a description of what I did and you might have better ideas. The main point is that you are aiming for the col between Derryclancy and Hungry Hill and that from the bridge the compass bearing is about 126° (a bearing that you won't be able to keep to for any distance).

Walk south-east from the bridge to cut out a loop of track and rejoin it to follow one of the above mentioned streams. When blocked by a long slab of rock, turn left to walk below it and so reach another stream. Follow this stream in turn uphill and when again blocked by crags leave it off to your right and continue the climb. At length the ground eases, crags are less formidable and it is an easy walk to the col through boggy terrain with the great lines of slabs on Hungry Hill well off to the right.

If in the course of all the foregoing mental and physical effort you have had time to absorb the scenery, you can't have failed to notice that it is magnificent: the splendid watercourses already described, between which are great crags and slabs and above all some of the highest and most majestic mountains in the peninsula.

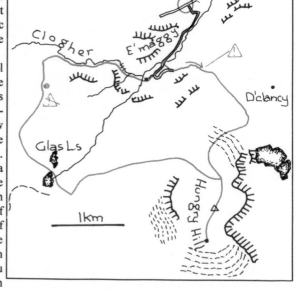

From the col Hungry Hill to the south-west looks dreadfully formidable: row upon row of grey sandstone guard this approach. Yet if you veer a little right of the direct line you can avoid nearly all of the hard work of surmounting these slabs and arrive on the summit plateau without too much effort.

Unfortunately the summit (685m) consists of a soggy plateau, about 1km long and a few hundred metres wide. Not at all what you would expect from the awesome ascent. Still, it is the highest point in the entire peninsula and if you wander first to the trig pillar (2.75 hours) at the centre of the plateau and then to the well-built cairn near the southern end you will enjoy great views in all directions, though not all from the same point.

When you have done all that return to the trig pillar, walk say 400m further north and then begin a long descent along an ill-defined rocky ridge ending at Caha Loughs 2km off to the west. This would be a difficult navigational task in bad weather were it not for the fact that, uniquely among Irish mountains there are paint marks all along this route from just off the summit plateau to Caha Loughs. So provided they are still visible and that you don't lose them, you can't go wrong. However, if either of these do not apply you could be in big trouble. Conclusion: take care and watch your step.

The paint marks take you all the way to just south of the large circular Caha Lough (3.75 hours), whose outlet stream you can follow in an emergency, at first gently then steeply downhill back to Glanmore (it's not an easy route so use it only if you must). The main route continues uphill for a few hundred metres to the north-west and then north and downhill along a stream. Diverting slightly from the stream takes you past a small circular lake, seemingly without inlet or outlet stream (the latter runs underground). Continue north from here to pick up the outlet stream shortly and so reach Clogher.

This is a high, flat and wet pastureland for sheep, a plain diversified by occasional rocky outcrops and the slowly meandering main stream with its numerous tributaries that cascade from the hillsides all around.

Well, almost all around - these streams have to exit somewhere. All you have to do now is follow the tributary stream you are at and then the main stream running east along the valley. Keep this main stream on the left and descend by the cascade that you saw on the initial ascent. Except during droughts this a most impressive watercourse, a wide steeply-angled slab carrying the stream's considerable volume of water (sketch, page 43). A steep descent, so take care.

When you reach the foot of the cascade continue along the stream to reach the nearby small copse. Here you will pick up the track you started out on and can walk directly to the start.

Hungry Hill by the Tourist Route: If you want to get to Hungry Hill with the minimum of effort, start at the highest point on the Healy Pass Road (GR 7853), where there are several places along the road in which you can park a few cars. The first few metres are steep over avoidable slabs, but after that the terrain is easy and as long as you keep the high ground on the right and do not wander initially onto a south-running spur you will easily climb Coombane (510m), from where Hungry Hill is visible for the first time, the mighty slabs across its face presenting a none too friendly visage.

Descend to the lake just beyond Coombane and then climb Derryclancy (554m). There is a gentle drop to the col facing Hungry Hill, from where it will be obvious that a detour to the right of the direct approach is advisable to avoid the worst of the lines of slabs on the direct route. Return by the same route. Walking time to the trig pillar is 2.5 hours (distance 5km, climb 540m, allowing about 15 minutes over Naismith to negotiate slabs) and 1.75 hours (140m climb and 15 minutes for slabs) on the return. ■

WEST AND SOUTH BEARA

The area covered here is the part of Beara Peninsula west of the N71 in county Cork. The focus of this area is undoubtedly Hungry Hill (routes 17, 18 - and route 10 above). Its summit plateau is far from imposing, but it is guarded on most flanks by great sandstone slabs, those to the east being particularly impressive. In stark contrast to Hungry Hill is the sharp cone of Sugarloaf (route 15), another excellent walking area. At the far west of the peninsula are low hills, some soggy, others with difficult slabs (route 16). Further east this contrast is exemplified by higher hills, soggy Maulin and slabby Knocknagree (route 13). Lastly there is excellent and not too demanding walking close to the thickly wooded area surrounding Glengarriff (routes 12, 14) and a short but difficult sea-cliff walk (route 11).

Sheep's Head Peninsula

ROUTE 11: KILCATHERINE POINT

Definitely a route for potterers and wanderers and not for the person who wants to cover ground. Memorable coastal and sea-cliff scenery with a wealth of interest for the nature lover so bring along binoculars and natural history books. And don't expect easy progress!

Getting There: The starting point is about 25 miles (40km) from Kenmare. Take the R571 to about 2 miles beyond Ardgroom. Turn right here, signposted 'Ardgroom 19km via Coast Road'. Drive for about 2 miles (3km) to pass a cemetery on the right and 0.8 miles further on park at a crossroads, with a track on the right, signposted for Ardgroom and Eyeries (GR 629536). This route may also be walked using the table 282 **bus** (just about).

Walking Time: This route is not really amenable to a precise time, because of the many features which will detain you willingly (flowers, seabirds etc) or unwillingly (difficult vegetation, rocks and short stretches of cliff). There's about 20 minutes easy walking on track and road at the start and about a half-hour's similar walk at the end. In between give yourself about 2 hours.

Difficulties: Navigation is easy; the terrain has already been copiously noted.

Map: Sheet 84 is hardly necessary. A small-scale map might be more useful to identify far-away features.

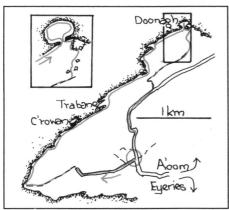

Route: From the crossroads walk west away from the track so taking a narrow road through an agricultural landscape of long grassy ridges. The road soon deteriorates to a track and ends with the island of Inishfarnard ahead. Here ends easy progress!

Turn right to follow the coast, though not rigidly as you will be diverted by the obstacles already mentioned and lots of items of interest. The first unmistakable feature is a tiny rocky island just off-shore shaped like a fish lying on its side (Carrigarowan on the map). Next, a few hundred lengthy metres farther on is a rectangular cove named Trabane, with large flat slabs seaward, a tiny grass plain landward. You may find the descent to the beach between these two exasperatingly difficult since it is guarded by short but steep slabs which you may, or may not be able to negotiate easily.

You can wander further along the shore, a place of long lines of slabs, low cliffs and occasional tiny cliff-bound inlets into which the sea whirls, until you come to a second island, Doonagh. Or maybe it isn't an island since it is joined to the mainland by a grassy arch. A good place to rest and have a bite.

From Doonagh you will be able to see further delectable stretches of coastline stretching ahead. It is possible to reach this stretch but it is a much tougher struggle than up to this, with fences, high and thorny vegetation and steep slabs running right into the sea. Rather than face all this is may be prudent to retreat.

To do so, head uphill and onward from Doonagh (with cliffs hereabouts there is little alternative) to reach a nearby field, the one and only hereabouts. Turn inland to follow its edge as far as a derelict house on the field's border. From here a little improvisation is needed, though only for a few hundred difficult metres until you hit a track. The idea is to contour round the hill initially south but swinging right, passing ruined houses until you see a track down on the left. Make your way painfully to it.

Turn right onto it and right again onto the road, which is to be followed all the way back to the start. There is a stiff climb to the crest where you will be rewarded by fine views seaward and over the Iveragh Peninsula to the north. Then it's downhill all the way. ∎

ROUTE 12: BARLEY LAKE

An exceptionally high start (290m) on a short route with dramatic views down into the heads of remote valleys to start and finish, with in contrast, a small-scale landscape of rocky outcrops, lakes and soft undulating ground in the plateau of the centre section.

Getting There: Take the N71 from Glengarriff, from where Barley Lake carpark (GR 879572) is close and well-signposted. From Kenmare take the N71 and turn right for Barley Lake just after the third (and last) tunnel along this road. Note if you are returning to Kenmare, that the signposting *from* Barley Lake is inadequate, so you should note the return route on the outward trip.

Walking Time: 2 hours (distance 5km, climb about 300m) but this can be easily extended.

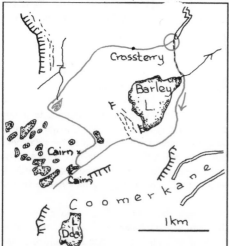

Difficulties: The main difficulty is a navigational one, that is finding the point at which to descend from the plateau at the end of the walk. Other than that, note that much of the ground on the plateau is soft and wet.

Map: Sheet 85.

Route: From the carpark take the well-worn path down to Barley Lake and cross its outlet stream. Walk south-west along its shore for a while, but since the goal is to reach the crest of the ridge off to the left, you will have to leave it after a while.. Head diagonally right upwards, using where possible one of a number of vague paths wandering through the rushy grass. As you ascend the ground becomes firmer and the going easier, so you will eventually attain the crest and can enjoy views of the valley of the Coomarkane River down on the left.

The one steep climb of the route lies at the end of this ridge. Descend to a narrow steep-sided col bridged by a stone wall. Here take the rough path beyond it steeply upward to the plateau called, a little oddly, Glenlough Mountain on the maps, since it doesn't seem to have much in common with glens, loughs or mountains. The plateau, which stretches for miles to the west and south, is undulating and boggy with rocky outcrops and numerous lakes: a small-scale, fascinating landscape in good weather and a bleak, anonymous, frightening desert in cloud.

You can wander to your heart's content around this plateau; the only real problem is getting off again, as there is much steep ground west of Barley Lake. The following is one not very adventurous route, which takes in some of the landmarks on the plateau.

Walk along the plateau edge, passing a cairn perched on a rough cube of rock at pt 471m, until you are reach a high point on the plateau edge a few hundred metres to the south-west. All along here you are looking down on the remote upper end of Coomarkane and beyond it the rugged summit of Sugarloaf. Return to the cairn and then walk to another cairn a short distance away to the north. From here it is worth walking parallel to long lines to slabs to reach the most easterly lake on the plateau, one by-passed on the ascent. The key to descending from the plateau lies directly north-west from here: the lake at about GR 863566. It might be some help to note that this lake is about 150m long (90 double paces) and has a rocky peninsula 20 to 30m long at its south-west corner.

From this lake walk north-east along a developing spur. As you advance you cannot fail to be impressed by the great lines of slabs at the head of the valley on the left, looking like the edges of the pages of a partly burnt book. After about 1km along the spur swing right into a lower boggy area after which comes the last slight climb onto the rocky but indistinct Crossterry Mountain (339m). Keep walking east to the nearby carpark. ∎

ROUTE 13: KNOCKNAGREE AND MAULIN

Two contrasting peaks, with Knocknagree a bold and rocky summit and Maulin a grassy plateau. With a track leaving only 180m climb to the summit of Knocknagree and a long, though not particularly easy stretch of the Beara Way to finish, this route offers a comparatively easy way to attain two of the highest peaks (586m, 621m) in the peninsula. The initial track can also be used to climb Hungry Hill.

Getting There: From Glengarriff, about 17 miles (27km) to the east, take the R752 through Adrigole, and park around the church on the right in Rossmackowen (GR 742472). Note that the sign heralding the village is placed a more than generous distance from the village centre itself. It may be possible to park about 0.6 miles uphill along the narrow road running north from the church but it is exceedingly narrow and parking is limited. Rossmackowen can also be easily reached from the Castletownbere direction.

Walking Time: 4.75 hours (distance 13km, climb 820m).

Difficulties: Some navigational headaches between Knocknagree and Maulin, otherwise easy. Terrain generally good.

Map: Sheet 84.

Route: Walk uphill on the narrow road which shortly deteriorates to a track. The Beara Way joins it for a short distance; continue upward on the track where the Way heads off to the left and farther up ignore unimpressive tracks heading off vaguely into bogland. From near the start you will see the great grey dome of Knocknagree ahead, while to the right views gradually open out to reveal the slabby western flank of Hungry Hill lording it over Comnagapple Glen and the oval of Park Lough.

After just over an hour's walking you will come to the highest point (and end) of the track overlooking the Glas Loughs. There should be paint marks and a path of sorts on the right heading for Hungry Hill - but we are Knocknagree-bound. Don't take a direct line to the summit; instead to avoid slabs and steep ground head well to the left to reach its southern spur and then head directly to the summit itself (1.75 hours).

From here pay some attention to navigation in an area not over-endowed with landmarks. Descend through minor slabs on Knocknagree's northern spur and then swing left to reach a small lake, bedecked with water-lilies and backed by steep slabs. This is in fact the last of slab country: from here on we are into soft boggy terrain with even the occasional herd of peat hags.

From the lake head directly west across high ground to reach a modest col between pt 579m to the north and Maulin (621m). Here head south to reach its unassuming summit, crowned by a tiny cairn marking the highest point in a long north-south quasi-plateau. Continue initially south along the crest of the gently sloping high ground, but gradually veer left off it to reach a minor track running

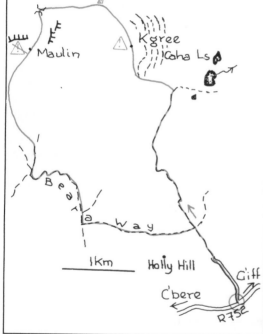

south (it looks more impressive on the map than it is). Walk straight ahead where this track meets a major track (it looks less impressive on the map than it is) and so join the Beara Way at waymark 79.

One of the more remote and scenic sections of the Beara Way is to be followed almost to the start so there should be no trouble with navigation. One caution: the OS map is completely incorrect in its depiction of the route. Ignore it.

Turn left at the waymark to descend on the track to upland fields in a remote valley, and turn right off it to cross the main stream in the valley on a sturdy bridge. Climb steeply to the crest of the spur just north of Holly Hill and descend directly to a track. It is of course the track on which you started, so all you have to do now is turn right downhill to the start. ■

ROUTE 14: LOUGH EEKENOOHOOLIKEAGHAUN

You're right - I couldn't resist such a name! And you will hardly be able to resist two delectable lakes (the other modestly called Derreenadarodia) set in the midst of towering crags and cliffs seemingly a thousand miles from anywhere, but in reality no distance from a tarred road. A short walk but from here you can easily walk onward to explore the area around Sugarloaf or Barley Lake.

Getting There: The start is about 3 miles (5km) from Glengarriff and you can bike it if you haven't a car. It's a lovely, wooded route nearly all the way from the town. Take the Castletownbere road (R572) over a wide bridge just outside the town, turn sharply right immediately after it (signposted for the Beara Way) and continue straight ahead, ignoring a turn on the right, to park shortly after by turning left off the main road and parking immediately on waste ground (GR 887558). **Buses:** 44, 46 to Glengarriff.

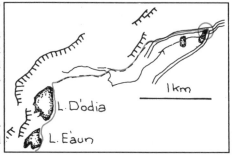

Walking Time: 2 hours (distance 6km, climb about 200m). However you could easily spend a half-day wandering around here.

Difficulties: None.

Map: Sheet 85, though unnecessary unless you want to extend the route (see below).

Route: Walk back to the main road, turn left and head into Coomerkane. After about 10 minutes walking turn right off what is now little more than a track onto what indubitably *is* a track. The track heads south-west under a massive cliff (try out its echo), and shortly reaches an easily fordable stream.

Take the rough path beyond into the upper reaches of the valley, passing great domes of rock off to the left and later on a shallow valley down on the right. The path ends just short of Lough Derreenadarodia and since there is a great spur of high, rocky land blocking a direct approach to the lake, you can either climb this spur or follow lower ground to the right to reach it. If you think this lake is scenic just wait till you get to Lough Eekenoohoolikeaghaun, reached by following the stream south between the two lakes.

This is an area for contemplation and leisurely pottering. You will find that a circuit of Eekenoohoolikeaghaun takes much longer than it reasonably should because of long tongues of steep rock around the lake which will cause several diversions.

Take the same route on the return. It is possible to make your way to the southern side of the valley and take the other tarred road in the valley to reach the start but several fences and less spectacular scenery make it not worth while.

Variations: By climbing from Eekenoohoolikeaghaun you can easily tackle Sugarloaf (route 15) or the Barley Lake (route 12) area. ∎

Sugarloaf is the near-perfect cone dominating Glengarriff from the west. The route starts from near the town on a remote section of the Beara Way before tackling the summit. The return is along a narrow ridge leading to a forest track. A rugged and varied route.

Getting There: From Glengarriff take the R572 for 2.2 miles (3.5km) to pass a religious statue on the left. Just beyond is a track sneaking off inconspicuously

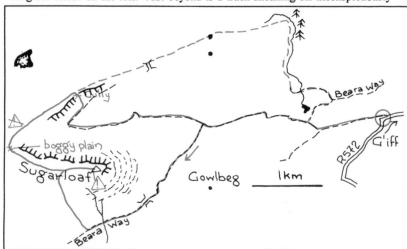

on the right. Park on the R572 around here (GR 914538), and *not* on the track. If you are without a car you can walk from Glengarriff, turn right on the Beara Way just past the caravan site and continue to the start proper. **Buses:** 44, 46 to Glengarriff.

Walking Time: 4.75 hours (distance 14km, climb 640m).

Difficulties: Navigation may cause anxious moments from the summit of Sugarloaf until the north-east spur is reached. The underfoot conditions on the variation are likely to be very trying.

Map: Sheet 85. The track shown running parallel to the north-east spur of Sugar Loaf does not extend as far as indicated.

Route: Take the track mentioned above initially through rough farmland, ignore the junction on the left and shortly after join the Beara Way at a waymark. Now in a country of rough tussocks, though mercifully still on the track, continue straight ahead to enter a birch wood. Shortly after emerging from it, follow the Beara Way off the track and uphill on a rough path. From here, as for some time previously, the great bulk of Sugarloaf rears ahead, falling in great cliffs to your right and with its long north-east running spur dominating the northern horizon.

The path reaches the top of the pass between Gowlbeg Mountain and Sugarloaf; you will know it because of low cliffs close on the left and the coast further off. You will see that if you try to tackle the peak from here you will have to climb a formidable series of slabs, not the easiest of approaches. So, walk about another 10 minutes and then turn right off the Way to climb a grassy slope hindered by only a few lines of slabs.

The task ahead is clear: climb resolutely upward. The lie of the land will dictate an initial climb north with a touch of west, but as you approach the summit you should swing to north-east. The summit (574m, 2.75 hours) has a trig pillar and, with cliffs dropping away at your feet and a whole array of lovely country stretching away in all directions is a marvellous viewpoint.

Keeping the cliffs on the right, descend to a narrow col and then ascend to a small area of rough, undulating country to its west, which has no definite summit and is thus most unhelpful terrain navigationally in bad weather. The (fairly) distinct landmark lying beyond is a boggy plain, perhaps 100m long, with its long axis reaching roughly north-east.

The idea now is to reach the long north-east running spur noted earlier. Contour cautiously north and then north-east from the plain for a few hundred metres, keeping steep ground on the right to reach it. Walk along the crest of the spur for about 1km, where you will note on the right of the crest (at about GR 871539) a fairly steep, grassy gully, bounded by crags, at the bottom of which are scattered trees. *This is the main route and the only easy way to descend.*

The rest of the route is easy, navigationally and underfoot. Descend the gully to reach a forest track a little way down, turn right onto it and take it through and out of forest. The track later forms part of the Beara Way and you should keep on the Way until it branches left. At this point retrace your steps to the start.

Difficult Variation: Much of this route is over tussocks and beds of grass into which you will sink slowly with every painful step. The total walking time is 6.5 hours (distance 15km climb 800m) including over an hour for these conditions.

Continue along the crest of the spur into terrain that becomes rougher and rockier (note that the trees shown on the map along the crest do not exist). The views are lovely: two long valleys to right and left, the former the one you toiled up earlier, the latter harbouring two attractive lakes (route 14). Ahead lies the next target, a small but impressive rocky pyramid (about 370m).

But before that the steady descent along the spur ends at a col where there is a junction of ancient fences. From here climb to the pyramid and prepare for the difficult terrain, that noted above. The idea is to continue along the spur for over a kilometre but veering gradually rightward away from its crest. This will mean that you should reach an area of scattered forest and a stream running south.

At the stream your troubles are far from over, though a track is only a few hundred metres away. The descent by the stream is similar to the terrain just encountered, with the added burden of a few short stretches of cliff to circumnavigate. It will probably be with some relief therefore that you see a field ahead and beyond it the start of a track.

The rest is easy. Lick your wounds, take the track to the Beara Way, turn right onto it, left off it at the next junction and left again to reach the nearby start. ■

ROUTE 16: KNOCKOURA AND KNOCKNAGALLAUN

In the far west of the Beara Peninsula looms a low L-shaped group of mountains, one leg stretching to boggy and dull Knockgour (481m). The other, the one the route follows, has rockier, steeper and craggier terrain and culminates in Knocknagallaun (376m). The views, mundane enough near at hand, are better towards the islands, headlands and rugged peninsulas of the coast.

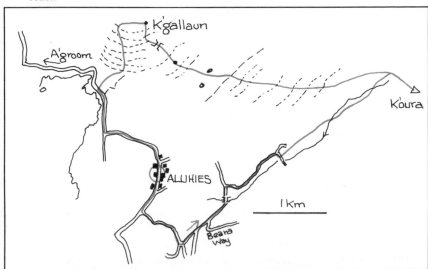

Getting There: Park in the village of Allihies (GR 5845) about 34 miles (55km) west of Glengarriff and 27 miles (43km) west of Kenmare.

Walking Time: 5.25 hours (distance 12km, climb 680m), thus allowing about three-quarters of an hour over Naismith for difficult slabs and a steep descent, all of which are in the second part of the route and can be avoided.

Difficulties: Increasingly rough terrain as the route progresses. As for navigation, watch out that you take the correct route at the start in a maze of tracks and narrow roads. Later, in open terrain, it is certainly possible to make navigational errors but civilisation is always close by, though you should take care over slabs and crags if you have to make an unscheduled descent.

Map: Sheet 84.

Route: From the start you can see the ridge to be climbed: it's the low, jagged hillside stretching east-west dominating the village from the north. It may be consoling to know that the terrain is not as rocky as it appears from here.

Take the Beara Way south from the village, that is away from the ridge, and turn left with it along a narrow track, and thence onto a narrow road traversing a countryside not enhanced by old mine workings and present day environmental carelessness. Where the Beara Way heads off uphill to the right continue on straight ahead to cross a bridge and shortly turn off onto a narrow road on the right, where a rusty shed may be some reassurance.

Things improve from here on. Follow the narrow road steadily uphill for 1km or so and just after the road swings right to the highest house on the hillside, cross the gate on the left (there's another gate directly opposite it), walk uphill through a field and beyond it through rough open ground, following an intermittent path. The views expand as you climb though the best are unfortunately behind. Near the crest of the hill you will be pushed right by crags so that you are eventually walking by the side of a swiftly running stream, thus affording easy, pleasant walking. Beyond the source of the stream however you will have to traverse a soggy area, an unpleasant reversal of fortune.

At the crest of the hill a whole panorama encompassing much of Iveragh, and including the jagged Reeks Ridge and lofty Carrauntoohil to its left opens out, a fitting reward for efforts so far. It is just about worthwhile ascending to the trig pillar on Knockoura to the south-east, though the boggy ridge south of Knockoura, worsened by an ugly track all the way to the TV masts on Knockgour, doesn't add to its attractions.

After returning to the point where you attained the crest of the ridge, the next stretch is the walk westward along it. As you do so you climb a series of indistinct summits on terrain which steadily becomes more rocky, rocky enough in fact to cause some diversions before you reach the highest point of a track, once again the Beara Way.

Here you can turn left and walk directly back to Allihies about 2km away. If you decide to complete the walk be warned that the terrain is a lot more rocky and steep from here on. OK? Cross the track and continue west along the crest of the spur towards Knocknagallaun, before which is a distinct drop into a deep col (it's too wide to qualify as a gully). After this you face a steep and craggy climb to the summit. You can opt out at this col by descending steeply south to pick up a stream but even if vertigo threatens on the ascent, you can veer to the left where the terrain is easier.

The summit (376m), though low, is the highest point seaward and therefore an excellent viewpoint. The two islands nearby at the tip of Iveragh to the north-west are cliff-bound Scariff and Deenish, while further off are the magical Skelligs. Having digested all this, it is time to consider the homeward route, which is a little tricky because of rocky terrain lower down the slope.

Start off west from the summit for a few hundred metres and then swing left over rocky terrain, looking out as you do so for a grassy ramp that will take you through the slabs. As you near the road, at this point close to the sea, you will encounter rough fields and the occasional house (since there is some building activity at the time of writing it is hard to be more exact) so you will have to study the terrain yourself and find an exact route to the road. Once there turn left and walk about 2km back to the village, a relaxing walk partly by the coast and partly through fields. ■

ROUTE 17: HUNGRY HILL FROM THE EAST

A most impressive approach to Hungry Hill: two lines of bare, rocky cliffs, one above the other, with two lakes perched precariously on the rough ground between them. The route outflanks these cliffs to their south, climbs through the slabs to the summit and descends to their north via Derryclancy. A short but tough walk and not recommended on days of low cloud.

Getting There: From Glengarriff take the R572 past Adrigole, specifically the junction of the Healy Pass Road. Less than a mile further on, pass a sign on the right for the waterfall, cross a bridge and immediately turn right. Drive for a further mile and park on waste ground on the right (GR 783493). **Bus** 46.

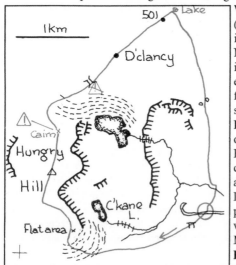

Walking Time: 5 hours (distance 10km, climb 800m) including a half-hour over Naismith to avoid slabs on the initial ascent and 15 minutes each for slabs on the descent from Hungry Hill and for the steep final descent.

Difficulties: Finding your way off the summit plateau of Hungry Hill is difficult in low cloud, with wide areas of cliff and slab in most directions. I'm speaking from painful personal experience! Keep this walk for a clear day.

Map: Sheet 84.

Route: Walk onward along the road, shortly crossing a stile on the left that leads into boggy country. Head upward and south-westward, evading further up the occasional harmless outcrop. As you climb the valley where you started opens out to reveal fields and the occasional clump of trees More dramatically, at the head of the valley the great cliffs and lines of slabs east of Hungry Hill look ever more daunting. That slender thread of waterfall, incidentally, zig-zagging its way into the valley, issues from Coomarkane Lake, which you will see later on.

At length you will reach the brow of the hill, perhaps at old turf workings. Here the view to the south opens out over Bear Island, snuggling in at the side of Bantry Bay. All very pleasant, but as you walk west along the crest your gaze will more likely turn towards the intimidating horizontal lines of slabs, stacked in a great pile, seemingly to the very summit of Hungry Hill.

If like me, you are a person of a nervous disposition you will not wish to tackle these slabs directly. Instead veer to the left to evade each unclimbable line, of which there are more than several. You will therefore find yourself eventually above Park Lough (by which a road runs) and climbing roughly north. On this course you will climb to a tiny flat area (at GR 764490) and be cheered to know that nearly all the slabs and most of the climbing to the summit is behind. In fact the well-constructed cairn near the south summit is only 100m climbing away.

Once on the south summit, navigation is easy and the ground, though a little soggy, allows easy walking. Walk to the trig pillar marking the highest point (685m), where you may be led to wonder if any mountain anywhere has a tamer summit compared to its ferocious flanks.

The descent to the col facing Derryclancy requires some care. Walk to the small cairn marking the north summit (at about 17° compass from the trig pillar). From here, instead of walking directly towards the col, which would take you over some horrific slabs, head well to the left of this (almost north-west) for a few hundred metres, and then swing about north-east. This admittedly makes navigation more difficult but avoids the worst of the slabs.

At the boggy col you will be able to admire Coomadayallig Lake down on the right below lines of slabs. You will view its memorable outlet stream later. For the moment climb through soft ground to the summit of Derryclancy (554m), a quite mundane affair: outcrops and a small lake, though the only one directly on the route so far.

Walk north-east from Derryclancy over rough country. The views are no better than have gone before (ie they are still magnificent), but now you can afford to concentrate on them. That's Glanmore Lake with its wooded islands down to the left, looking particularly impressive from here.

The next landmark to look out for is the lake just beyond pt 501m, and this is again the largest lake encountered so far. This marks the point where you can divert off the ridge running towards Healy Pass and head for home. Walk south with a touch of east, towards the soggy plateau of Derreen, specifically heading for a couple of small lakes set on the plateau's edge. On the right across the valley you will see a waterfall thundering down from Coomadayallig Lake over cliffs and crags, and the occasional clump of thick vegetation sheltering in unapproachable rocky crevices. Quite a sight.

Descend south from the lakes, veering left if slabs or steep ground proves too difficult. Once on level ground, cross the wide and therefore fordable river just upstream of the border between rough ground on the left and cultivated fields on the right and opposite a gate bearing an unfriendly sign. With this warning firmly in mind, walk a few metres downstream and then climb upwards through the rough ground to inspect a massive stone circle close to the road, before reaching the start. ■

This approach along the stern rocky ground between the two sets of cliffs marking the eastern side of Hungry Hill gives breath-taking views of cliff, mountain lake and plunging waterfalls. In addition it leaves you with the option of climbing Hungry Hill if you wish.

Getting There: Start at the same place as route 17.

Walking Time: 3.5 hours (distance 7km, climb 680m), thus allowing about a half-hour over Naismith for difficult terrain and one fairly steep descent.

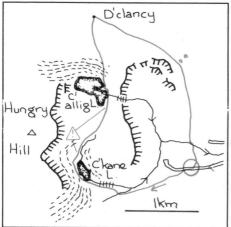

Difficulties: Some moderately difficult navigation and wicked cliffs after Coomarkane Lake so be very wary about going further on bad days.

Map: Sheet 84.

Route: Walk onward along the road, shortly crossing a stile on the left. Continue diagonally right uphill watching out on the right for a stream cascading in zig-zags around great slabs. Head gradually for it crossing a minor stream on the way, which you will not mistake for the one with the cascades.

Whatever about the terrain, you need not worry about navigation when you reach the cascade: just follow it uphill. You may be diverted here and there by boulders and mighty sheets of slab along the stream's course but you will soon pick it up again. At length the slope relents and a few more hundred metres brings you to Coomarkane Lake. What a location! Great bare cliffs reaching to Hungry Hill to the left, wild and rough rocky ground in other directions with the lake itself occupying a hollow in a narrow strip of boggy ground.

From Coomarkane Lake a compass bearing is highly advisable to take you safely to Coomadayallig Lake to the north, specifically to its eastern shore. You will initially follow the course of a stream uphill to its source and beyond it drop through rough ground to Coomadayallig. Much larger than Coomarkane, and with a small island to which a narrow peninsula reaches, it is in not quite so impressive a location as Coomarkane though the cliffs on the left are equally stern. This lake is also the source of the water for a waterfall seen towards the end of the walk, though it would require heroic disregard for life and limb to see more than the quickening stream from this location.

Talking of this heroic disregard: if you look west across the lake from the peninsula you will see one (and only one) gully which looks as if it might offer an easy route to the summit of Hungry Hill. *I haven't attempted it!*

The next target is Derryclancy. From the peninsula walk only a few hundred metres farther along the shore (beyond this slabs make progress difficult) and then climb directly to Derryclancy (554m), a dull mound but with superb views. You can lengthen the walk from here by walking to Coombane (route 17), but let's assume that you are homeward bound.

Descent from Hungry hill (Route 10)

Walk south-east from the summit for over 1km, heading for two small lakes at the southern end of a gently sloping soggy plateau. Though highly visible from afar, you may have difficulty finding the lakes from near at hand because they are tucked into rocky knolls on the plateau's edge. From the lakes head south fairly steeply downhill. Along here you can admire the high waterfall plunging from Coomadayallig Lake, whose source you couldn't see previously.

As you descend watch out ahead across the main river in the valley for the border between rough ground (left) and fields (right). Cross the river opposite a gate near this border; the water level is usually so low that you can wade across without trouble. Walk a few metres downstream to the corner of the rough ground and ascend from here to the road, passing on the way a massive standing stone close to the start, which is well worth a slight diversion to inspect. ■

SUMMARY OF APPROACHES TO HUNGRY HILL

Working clockwise from the north the main approaches to Hungry Hill are:
From Glanmore using the end of route 10 in reverse.
From Glanmore (the start of route 10). Not recommended on the return.
From the top of the Healy Pass Road (route 10, variation). An easy approach.
From the east near Adrigole (routes 17 or 18). If using route 18 beware of severe slabs north of Coomdayallig.
From just east of the church in Rossmackowen there is a signposted route.
From the church in Rossmackowen using the start of route 13.

SOUTH KERRY (EXCEPT BEARA)

To avoid infringing too far into the territory covered by *Hill Walkers Kerry*, this section is confined to the southern sides of the mountains of Iveragh and the mountains in county Kerry to their east. This latter area is admittedly defined simply by the county boundary rather than any inherent topographical unity.

The mountains on the south of Iveragh covered by this book (routes 21, 23) are a lovely area for walking that offers near views of the impressive Reeks.

The area encompassing the mountains of Kerry east of Iveragh is lower than that farther west. There are gently sloped, remote hills (route 19), and others even more remote with rougher terrain partly split by long, deep, fertile valleys (routes 20, 22). These last two routes are in parts over rough ground and, though it is not obvious from the maps, there are unexpected crags on their flanks which means that the end of routes in particular are not all that straightforward. With this (significant!) proviso this is an excellent area for leisurely exploration.

ROUTE 19: THE PAPS

The aptly named Paps, located to the east of the main ranges of Kerry, offer wide and impressive views though they themselves are not over-exciting, with bland slopes and only modest corries and lakes on their northern sides. The quiet roads and tracks on the south are much more attractive than those of the north and so it is from this side that the route approaches the twin summits.

Getting There: Take the N22 from Killarney, pass the junction of the R567 and turn left after another mile (1.6km) (signposted 'Clydagh Valley'). Drive onward for another 2.7 miles (4.3km) to park around the turn on the left (GR 144840). If coming from the Cork direction please avoid the alternative shorter road into the Clydagh Valley as it is very narrow.

Walking Time: 3 hours (distance 7km, climb 580m).

Difficulties: Some prickly vegetation near the end. Navigation is easy.

Map: Sheet 79.

Route: Take the track running north at the junction. It climbs into remote mountain country, more remote even than that on the drive through the Clydagh

Valley. There is initially forestry on the left and where it ends, and here the track is running almost on the level, leave it and climb at first through high heather directly to the summit, taking advantage of sheep paths where obliging.

There is a huge tomb on the summit of the East Pap (694m, 1.5 hours) and the views, where not blocked by the West Pap, whither (of course) the best views

Slab Country Around Sugarloaf (Route 15)

lie, are excellent. Descend west to the nearby col, admiring as you do so the mighty cliffs towering above Lough Nageeha tucked into the cleavage (as it were). You will also note a curious line of near-vertical slabs climbing the north side of the West Pap; whether natural or man-made I know not.

Ascend steeply by these slabs to the West Pap (690m) from where the views to the Reeks are unsurpassed. The descent south over low heather is easy. Keeping to the crest of the spur you will climb slightly to pt 622m and then reach Rodger's Rock, the crags and rocks a few hundred metres to the south.

From Rodger's Rock you might like to consider how to reach the road to the south. You will see below you two forestry plantations with a copse of pines between them and a rough field fronting the road to the copse's right. *One way* of reaching the road is to descend from the Rock through high heather so as to reach the near corner of the copse. Then veer right into the field (the direct approach to the field is barred by high gorse). Cross *carefully* onto the road at a point where the roadside earthbank is breached. If for some reason you don't fancy this approach you could head to the near corner of the plantation on the left and follow the stream here down to a track ending on to the road. Neither of these approaches to the road is child's play, so it might be some relief to reach it and walk without fear of barriers the 1km back to the start.

Easy Variation: From the starting point above you can walk east (onward) on a secluded road or track into Clydagh Valley for about 6km. In spite of having to return by the same route this is a lovely, varied walk. ■

ROUTE 20: PRIESTS LEAP AND BARRABOY

A generally easy route in the form of a great triangle. The initial side is on narrow road, and the second over rugged country centred on the fine slab-sided cone of Barraboy (about 460m), not the highest but certainly the most striking mountain on the route. For the third side you have a choice: the Beara Way on track and road or a broad high spur ending in a steep descent avoiding crags.

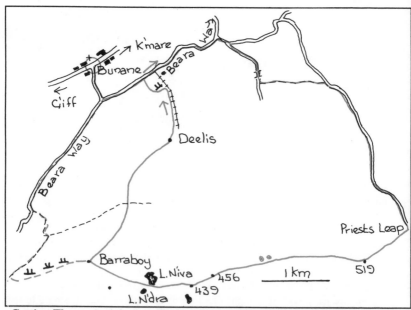

Getting There: Park in the village of Bunane (GR 9363) on the N71 about 10 miles (15km) north of Glengarriff and 6 miles (10km) south of Kenmare.

Walking Time: 5.75 hours (distance 17km, climb 720m), with difficult terrain counterbalanced by road-walking.

Difficulties: Some terrain lacking in definite features and so not too easy to navigate over, though mistakes should not be too punishing After reading this, you won't find the crags at the end of the route so unexpected.

Map: Sheet 85.

Route: The first 1½ hours of this walk is on road or track, but is not without its attractions. The first stretch follows the Beara Way. Take it south from opposite the church, turn left at the tee and if you intend to do the hard variation (see below) watch out after about 5 minutes from the tee for a suitable cragless place on the right to descend to the road - it shouldn't be difficult. For the moment continue along the road through pleasant sylvan countryside to cross a bridge after which the Way turns left. Here turn right, shortly fork right to cross a bridge and take the next turn left. Turn right at the tee. And now in an area of good farming land with rolling mountainside farther away you will be glad to hear that complicated instructions are over for a while!

Now on a narrow road, we face much more remote country. Continue onward and upward on it, with initially on the left a broad grassy basin devoid of the works of man. Then the road crosses over the crest of a spur; here a considerable area of mountain greets the rightward-flung eye, and yes, we are going to climb much of it.

The highest point on the road is called Priests Leap, and is a spectacular viewpoint considering that it is from a road, with Bantry and a large area of county Cork away to the south. You might as well walk a few metres down the road on the Cork side to inspect the rock from which the eponymous leap took place. Marked by a cross, it is highly unimpressive.

Time to leave the comfort of civilisation. Turn right (south-west) off the road and roughly following a meandering fence climb pt 519m. Then swing west to reach an indistinct col with two small lakes which might act as minor landmarks. From here climb pt 456m which, with pt 439m forms a virtual plateau. Along here you can see to the west the great corrie holding Barley Lake with the sharp cone of Sugarloaf to its left and the great plateau of Hungry Hill looming behind.

There hasn't been much navigational comfort so far since leaving the road. However, from the plateau the sizeable (and therefore distinct) Lough Nagarriva lies ahead. Better still you should be able to see the great slabs rising diagonally to the summit of Barraboy itself close to the west, the next major target.

But first Lough Nagarriva. From the plateau aim between it and Lough Namaddra, thus avoiding a most awful terrain of boulders on the east side of Nagarriva. From the south-western side of the lake head directly to Barraboy (over 460m) which is coincidentally the same height as Priests Leap. Not much altitudinal progress for so much work!

At Barraboy you have a choice. In bad visibility, with the prospect of indistinct terrain ahead, I suggest you take the navigationally easy route, which involves about 4km in all on track or narrow road. Simply descend roughly west on the crest of the spur to reach the Beara Way again, at forest on a high pass. Turn right here and take the Way down through initially remote and wild country to a three-way signpost near Bunane, where you turn left for the village,

The harder route follows the indistinct broad spur north-east from Barraboy, crosses over a track at a soggy col, where you can turn left to meet the Beara Way if you want a last-minute reprieve. If not climb north-east to Deelis (about 370m) which has no distinct top in a rough plateau of bog and outcrop. After it descend north following a fence through moorland, which is so bland and innocent underfoot that you would never think that all could end in tears at the nasty crags facing the road.

As you reach the first of these crags, and having studied the terrain earlier in the day, you will know to contour left (south-west) from the fence for only 200m or so to reach steep but safe grassy ground. Descend directly to the road (you shouldn't have to cross a fence), turn left on it, walk the few hundred metres to the three-way signpost and turn right here for Bunane. ■

ROUTE 21: MANGERTON

The views down into the spectacular corrie lakes etched into the northern side of the dull Mangerton plateau are the highlight of this route, as they would be of any route in Ireland. Before and after this is a steady climb and descent to and from the plateau, with the long ascent enlivened by a fascinating area of lake and crags south-west of the plateau.

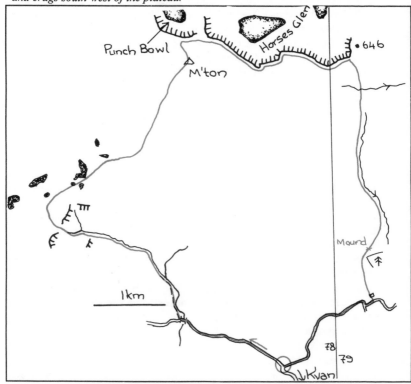

Getting There: From *Kilgarvan* take the road towards Kenmare for a short distance, pass the church on the right in the town and 0.5 miles (0.9km) beyond it take a turn on the right that bends sharply back. From *Kenmare* pass the Quill Centre as you enter Kilgarvan and take the next turn left. In both cases drive onward, keeping to the 'main' road for 2.6 miles (4.2km) to park at a tee (GR 993766). Parking is limited here so it may be better to turn right and park considerably on waste ground along that branch.

Walking Time: 5.5 hours (distance 15km, climb 780m).

Difficulties: Some rough ground, but navigation generally easy.

Map: Sheets 78 and 79 with an easy transition between the two.

Route: From the tee turn left (north-west) to walk along the narrow road through agricultural land with Mangertonbeg to the left and the 'big brother' filling the northern skyline. After about 1.5km (less than 20 minutes) cross a bridge and shortly after take a track on the right close to a stream. Where the track shortly expires keep to this stream to avoid dreadful tussocks if you leave it. The stream has two main tributaries: make sure you take the left-most one whose source is off to the west.

At length you will pass on the left the first of many rocky crags. Just beyond it two tributaries converge. Take the minor one, which is falling eastward, and beyond its source climb through steep and rocky ground between even steeper and rockier ground on both sides.

After much toil you will reach the plateau to the west. This is the area of tiny lakes, precariously positioned erratic rocks and short but stern crags mentioned in the introduction to this route. You can wander round here to your heart's content, but as you do make sure your general direction is north-east, whence Mangerton itself beckons.

This memorable area comes to an abrupt end as you walk north-east and face the steady climb to the summit of Mangerton over bleak moorland. The only consolation are the views opening up (though they were already excellent) with the Reeks and the other mountains of Iveragh to the west, the mountains of Beara to the south-west and many more gentle hills to the south and east.

Mangerton (843m, 3.25 hours) has a trig pillar; otherwise you would have to guess you were at the summit, so gently sloping is the moorland around. Walk north-west for 300m from here for a quite different terrain, for now you are standing on the rim of the corrie called the Devil's Punch Bowl, its lake over 150m below you. Quite a sight, and one that will intensify as you walk onward for the next 2km or so.

Turn right at the corrie edge to pass in turn the arete between the Bowl and Lough Erhogh, then the cliff edge above Erhogh and finally that above the farther away Lough Managh (the valley below, the Horses' Glen, takes a strange right-angle bend between Erhogh and Managh). Navigation is easy but in poor visibility you might watch out for two abrupt changes in direction in the cliff edge, both above Lough Erhogh: one of only a few metres, the other of over 100m. You will be walking away from the cliff edge where it swings irrevocably north, but neither of these two northward swings are that point.

When you do reach it (in good visibility when you don't need it Stoompa to the north is a good indicator) turn south away from the cliffs and cross the headwaters of an eastward-running stream. Continue onward to meet the headwaters of another stream, this one running south. Keep it on your left (if you like you can of course keep to the higher ground farther west).

As you descend through grazing land you will see forest ahead. Aim roughly for its right corner (there's a navigationally reassuring grassy mound at it), but ensure that you have all major tributaries on the left. From about this corner head south to reach a nearby gate. Cross it and continue south to pass a sadly derelict house. Turn right onto the road at the end of its driveway and right again at the nearby tee. All that remains now is to walk over a kilometre on minor roads roughly south-west to the start. ∎

With the notable exception of the stiff climb to the summit of Gullaba Hill this is an easy walk through varied lowland - deciduous trees, farmland and remote moorland - and an upland featuring the rims of two corries, one of which holds a large scenic lake.

Getting There: From *Kilgarvan* take the road south signposted for Bantry, turn right shortly thereafter at the tee where there is no signpost, drive another mile or so to pass a sign for Macaura's grave, and turn right after another 0.7 miles. Drive 0.3 miles to park around a track running straight ahead where the road swings right (GR 013700). If you need plenty of parking you can drive onward to a tee, turn left and park shortly on waste ground on the right. From *Glengarriff* you will probably have to over-shoot the correct turning, go on to the sign for the grave and return. **Buses:** 44 (express), 270 (local) to Kilgarvan.

Walking time: 4.5 hours (distance 13km, climb 680m).

Difficulties: The steep climb to Gullaba has already been noted. There is one river to cross at the start that may present problems after heavy rain and terrain towards the end without clear landmarks, but this is an area from where you can easily and safely find your way down.

Map: Sheet 85 with a tiny piece on sheet 79 that you can safely ignore.

Route: Take the track mentioned above through a lovely deciduous wood, pass a derelict house and shortly after cross two streams, the first of which may cause a little bother. After this continue on the track heading very roughly south, though with many twists and turns, out of forest into upland fields and eventually to its end directly below the north-east face of Gullaba.

Contour onward for a few hundred metres, avoiding gorse bushes as you do to you reach a stream. Ford it in order to avoid crags and even worse underfoot conditions on the other side and prepare for some hard climbing, the idea being to reach the col between Bird Hill (on the left) and Gullaba (on the right).

Having reached boggy country on the near side of the col you may not be too pleased to learn that another climb lies (or rather towers) ahead. Cross the stream and walk away from it for a short distance to reach the only tree hereabouts (though planting looks to be in the offing) and you will find yourself at the foot of a long, steep gully. If you climb it you will at least evade the crags in the area and eventually find yourself at the summit of Gullaba in one piece.

Gullaba (about 600m) commands views right down the Beara Peninsula to the south-west, the pyramid of Mullaghanattin to the west, the Reeks to the north-west, and the great plateau of Mangerton to the north, as well as a whole range of lesser peaks in other directions. I hope it was worth the pain of the ascent.

Walk south to pt 625m, on the way keeping to the left of the crest of the spur to view the road far below snaking upwards on its way to Bantry and later, as you climb towards the summit, an impressive corrie also on this side.

Another and even more impressive corrie lies ahead, that holding Coom-clogherane Lake. Walk west from pt 625m to the nearby corrie rim, where you can view an unlikely area of lush grass and an impressive boulder field perched on a steep slope down the corrie wall. Follow the rim, keeping it on the right as you walk clockwise partly round the lake. This route will take you first west, then fairly steeply downhill to the north-west before tackling the craggy pt 449m, which is crowned by an impressive assembly of rocks. You will note, by the way, that there has been considerable planting and track construction on the valley floor to the north and east of Coomclogherane Lake, none of which appears on the map.

Having climbed pt 449m you may well wish to head for home as the rest of the route is over not very inspiring country. If so descend north-west to the nearby col and then north-east over rough ground to reach a forest track. Turn left on it and right on tarmac to reach the start (but see also below).

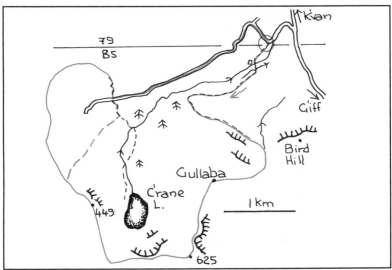

If however you want to go on, walk down to the aforementioned col, and then climb to boggy country to its north. Swing right to keep to the high ground, so walking well above the highest house in the valley and passing the ends of two bog tracks serving the plentiful turf-cutting operations hereabouts. Along here you will be modestly rewarded by views of Kenmare to the west as well as new angles on the high mountains of Iveragh.

Once you are past the highest house you can take the next and last bog track down to tarmac. Turn left here and walk steadily downhill through upland fields, rough grazing and new forestry. After 2km or so on the road you will pass a transmitter station and know to turn right shortly after for the start. ■

ROUTE 23: BOUGHIL
The line of modest hills stretching east to west from Boughil (639m) to Knocklomena (641m) run parallel to Broaghnabinnia and its eastern ridge and also to the mighty Reeks; westward is the lofty pyramid of Mullaghanattin. In spite of being overshadowed by more lofty summits this easy undulating ridge

walk offers the ambience of the high hills as well as excellent views in most directions.

Getting There: From Kenmare take the N71 northwards towards Killarney, branching left onto the R568 at Moll's Gap. Drive 3.7 miles (5.9km) along the R568 to park at a rudimentary and inconspicuous forest entrance on the right.

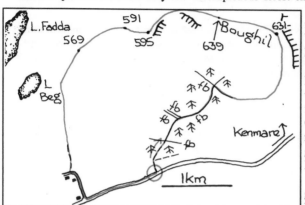

Take care not to miss it!

Walking Time: 4 hours (distance 10km, climb 760m)

Difficulties: Rough, wet ground underfoot to start. Otherwise easy and not too difficult navigation.

Map: Sheet 78 or 1:25 000 "Macgillycuddy's Reeks".

Route: The initial route from the forest entrance, as described hereafter, sounds dreadfully complicated. However all you really have to do is climb steadily for less than a half-hour until you find a clearing in the forest on the right leading to the base of Boughil itself. The details in the next paragraph are only if you want to be sure of exiting from forest at the right place (or *a* right place).

Take the rough track from the forest entrance, ignore a minor turn on the right, and continue straight ahead at a firebreak crossing your track. At this point the track, which up to this had a barely recognisable surface, degenerates to a firebreak of high tussocks. Farther up you will pass a firebreak crossing yours and a firebreak immediately after on the left only. At the next firebreak, this one crossing yours, turn right to reach young forest and just beyond it the start of the climb to Boughil, all this being clearly visible as you turn.

Work your way east to open country and then climb directly to Boughil (631m). Once there the route ahead, in clear visibility anyway, is simplicity itself. Walk west to Boughil (639m), where you will pick up a fence or a line of boundary stones which continues most of the way to pt 569m (but not beyond it) thus constituting a useful life-line should navigation fail.

After Boughil (639m) drop into a shallow col with fine cliffs on the left edging a narrow indentation in the range. Then climb steeply to the plateau running west from pt 595m through pt 591m to pt 569m. If you have any doubts about your location in this area you only have to walk a little farther west to see one or both of two lakes, the unimaginatively named Fadda (long) and Beg (small).

From pt 569m head south with a touch of east to reach the upper end of a gradually widening path heading south to houses screened by groups of trees. At its lower end at the houses turn left onto a wide track. Turn left again onto the road to reach the start less than 1km away. ∎

WEST CORK (EXCEPT BEARA)

This region covers a great arc of country running from the smaller peninsulas at the south-west tip of Ireland northwards through hill country on the borders of Kerry. Here the best known area is Gougane Barra (route 29), which boasts stern crags and slabs surrounding a popular lake. Routes 26 and 27 have similar terrain to Gougane Barra, though they lack such a lake and are much remoter.

The Sheep's Head and Mizen Head peninsulas (routes 24, 25) offer good sea-cliff walking as well as short hill walks. Inland are areas of modest mountains giving easy walking and views of rich upland valleys, broad river basins and wooded, undulating country (routes 28, 30).

ROUTE 24: MIZEN HEAD

Excellent views of a remote lighthouse set among mighty sea-cliffs, sections of which are crumbling under relentless pounding from the waves. The walk continues inland to give a higher view of the jagged Cork coastline.

Getting There: Leave the N71 just south of Bantry (26 miles, 42km away) to take the R591 to Goleen or leave the N71 at Ballydehob to take the R592 and later the R591 to Goleen. In Goleen follow signs for Mizen Head. Park in the Visitor Centre for the lighthouse (GR 739235). **Bus** 46 to Goleen.

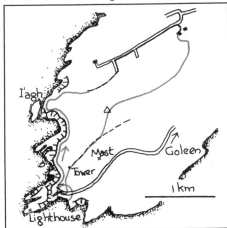

Walking Time: 2.5 hours (distance 7km, climb 300m).

Difficulties: One stretch of rough ground, otherwise easy.

Map: Sheet 88 is hardly needed.

Route: Walk to the far end of the carpark, but rather than take the narrow road towards the Centre take the gate to its right. Walk the track beyond to its nearby first bend and continue straight ahead here on any section of available path with the aim of reaching the sea-cliffs roughly off to the west (sorry, it's impossible to be more precise). In spite of this vague direction you should shortly find yourself above the lighthouse and with the disused Signal Tower to the right.

From here all is simple navigationally for some time. Lush grass underfoot, majestic sea-cliffs running from your feet in a contorted line ahead, scolding sea-birds sweeping oceanwards - this is a section on which to dawdle. After about 1km of slow convoluted walking from the lighthouse you will arrive at the off-shore island of Illaunnacaheragh; you will have to walk close to the cliff edge to confirm its insular status. From here on the cliffs are not so dramatic and attention turns inland. A few hundred metres beyond Illaunnacaheragh watch out for a farmhouse across the fields directly inland and walk to the end of the track just to its right. Take this track to tarmac and turn right to walk it through agricultural land. After about 1km turn right onto the second driveway on this side. To avoid disturbing the occupants in the two houses here, cross the first gate on the right, and make your way directly to the top of the first field. At about its mid-point cross into rough ground.

The plan now is to attain the crest of the hill to your south and the plan of the high vegetation around here seems to be to prevent your so doing. Perhaps the best idea is to climb diagonally left, though when you get there you may think otherwise. Somehow (I hope) you will reach the crest and have easy terrain running south-west to Mizen Head (232m) with excellent views in all directions. From the trig pillar marking the summit walk to the prominent mast to the south and from there back to the carpark. ■

ROUTE 25: SHEEP'S HEAD PENINSULA

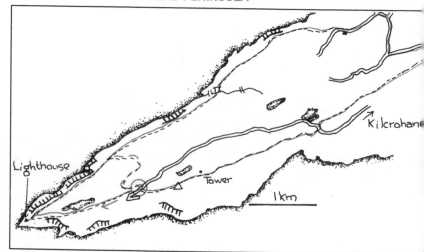

This route, mostly on the waymarked Sheep's Head Way, is at the remote end of the peninsula where it is bounded by great sea-cliffs. Inland long slivers of grey rock shelter rough grassland and a wealth of plants. This is an area for pottering, so take your time and you should find it greatly rewarding.

Getting There: Not the easiest place in the world to get to. From Bantry (21 miles, 34km away) take the N71 south (Cork-wards), branching gently right shortly after Bantry House. Keeping to the main road drive along the north side of the peninsula and eventually over its spine to reach the village of Kilcrohane. Turn right here and drive to near the end of the road at Tooreen (GR 733341) where there is plenty of room to park and a charming lady to dispense tea, coffee and goodies. **Bus** 255 to Kilcrohane.

Difficulties: Much rough ground but navigation is easy since the whole route is waymarked or on road and track. Don't fall over cliffs!

Walking Time: Difficult to say and hardly relevant in a pottering area. The total distance is about 14km and the climb about 400m. Allow at least a half-day if you want to do the whole route, though it may easily be shortened.

Map: Sheet 88 is hardly necessary. It shows the Way exceptionally badly.

Route: Follow the Way westward, first on tarmac and then along a rough path. You might like to leave this path by diverting left from it and so gain a view of massive sea-cliffs. Thus you can wander as far as the lighthouse or indeed even further west over boulders and crags to reach the very end of the peninsula, where you might see whales and dolphins in the late summer and autumn.

Lough Napeasta (Route 7)

Retrace your steps to the lighthouse and continue north-east, cliffs on the left. You have plenty of choice in this initial route from the lighthouse: sea-cliffs, land-cliffs or a shallow valley between them. Just after a narrow cove backed by mighty cliffs you will, if you are now on the Way, reach the start of a waymarked route back (it will take about 20 minutes). However if you have the time it is well worth going on though the sea-cliffs are not so dramatic. Eventually you will be channelled back to the Way at a stile at about GR 743354, where there is a good place for a rest at a stream that tumbles seaward in a set of small waterfalls.

Continue onward still roughly following the Way for another 2km, until you are eventually on a road set among fields. Time to cross the peninsula and rejoin the Way on the other side. Where the Way turns left keep on the road to walk upward to the crest of the hill, turn left here, walk the road for less than a kilometre, then turn first right at a house onto a track to rejoin the Way.

The Way is to be followed west to the start and detailed directions are not needed. In contrast to the outward leg the views here, on the modestly elevated spine of the peninsula, are to the neighbouring peninsulas, Beara to the north and Mizen Head to the south. The route is a mixture of path, rough track and a tiny section of road. After passing the highest point on the route, a modest 239m at the trig pillar, descend to the parking place where you will have well earned the refreshments on offer there. ∎

ROUTE 26: CAOINKEEN CLIFFS AND KNOCKBOY

The massive overhanging cliffs of Caoinkeen dominating tree-enclosed Lough Akinkeen and the remote Borlin valley make the two focal points for this route, rather than lofty Knockboy (706m). In between the underfoot conditions vary from easily forgettable bogland to memorable and demanding crags and slabs.

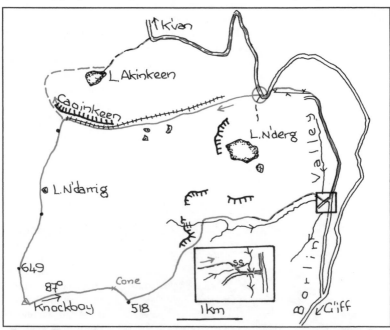

Getting There: From *the north* let's say you enter Kilgarvan (GR 0073) from the Kenmare direction. Pass a church on the left. Take the next right, signposted 'Bantry 35km'. Turn right shortly where there is no sign and continue straight ahead for about 8 miles (13km) to pass a sign indicating the Cork border. Park a little further on at the crest of the hill where there is a track on the right and room for several cars to park considerately (GR 039649).

From *Glengarriff* take the N71 towards Bantry, cross a bridge after 6 miles (9km) and turn immediately left signposted 'Kilgarvan 17km'. Drive onward for another 7 long miles (11km) until you come to a sign asserting 'Kilgarvan 17km' (yes, I know) and if you have two cars turn left here and park one opposite the nearby stone circle. Drive onward on the main road with the second (or only car) to park at the crest of the hill at the track on the left.

Walking Time: 4.75 hours (distance 13km, climb 750m) assuming one car.

Difficulties: Navigation is far from easy over the rumpled terrain after Knockboy, though mistakes should not be disastrous. The variation avoids this area - and much of the best scenery. Some difficult terrain underfoot.

Map: Sheet 85. The map incorrectly names a small side valley at about GR 0463 as the Borlin Valley. In fact, the Borlin Valley runs north-south on the left for much of the road north from Glengarriff.

Route: Head south-west on a broad spur, keeping to the left of the crest for a while to view Lough Nambrackderg beneath cliffs on one side and with a sea of conifers creeping up on the other. Beyond it you can follow a fence past one small lake and then two small ones hiding among the rocky outcrops hereabouts. After that, and still following the fence, the great cliffs of Caoinkeen become increasingly dominant to the west until you can stand poised right above them to view Lough Akinkeen way down below. At this point you are standing on a truncated summit at about 680m, confusingly called Knockboy on the maps, confusing because you are about to tackle a higher Knockboy 3km off to the south.

Walk south from the cliffs to the impressive summit cairn and from there descend over dull terrain to the peat hags around Lough Nambrackdarrig. Emerging from among the hags you should encounter a small lake not shown on the map and from there ascend to a rocky hillock, pt 649m. There is only a minimal descent before climbing once again to the trig pillar on Knockboy (706m, 2.5 hours), the highest point reached of any in this book, though far from the most memorable. The views however are most impressive with the sharp cone of Mullaghanattin evident to the west with the Reeks, the great plateau of Mangerton and the aptly named Paps running successively to its east.

Take care on the descent from Knockboy. From the summit you should see the next target, a small but striking rocky cone at GR 017623 about 1km away at the left end of a rocky spur (the compass bearing to it is 87°). Descend from the trig pillar over rough grassy ground and the occasional avoidable minor crags to cross flat bogland and climb slabs to the summit of this cone. From there climb to the nearby indistinct pt 518m to the south-east.

After this you have a choice. The general idea is to reach the side valley to the north-east, 'Borlin valley' on the OS map. You can, as I did, walk to the headwaters of one of the valley's streams, avoiding tussocks as best you can. Then cross the head of the valley to reach the area downstream of a waterfall cascading into the valley. This suggestion is only one of several which are evident from the map, but it does solve early the problem of crossing the main stream in the valley.

From this remote and lovely location head east along the valley floor to pick up a rough track. Keep on it to cross the river of the side valley on stepping stones and just beyond them turn left onto a narrow road. At the nearby tee turn right to reach one car, that is if you took two.

If your one and only car is at the crest of the hill off to the north then there is nothing for it but to walk there. At the tee mentioned above turn left and walk along the narrow country road, past the occasional neat farmhouse, for this area is exceptionally tidy, until the road swings west at the head of the valley. Here roughly follow the electricity pylons steeply uphill, a matter of 250m climb at the end of the walk and hardly to be welcomed in spite of the lovely views of the valley behind you. The car is a the crest of the hill - I hope so anyway!

Easy Variation: Take the main route as far as the Caoinkeen cliffs and continue initially west to descend to the north of Lough Akinkeen. Here you will pick up a track ending on the road. Turn right and walk uphill on the road to the crest of the hill. Total walking time is 3.25 hours (distance 9km, climb 480m). ■

ROUTE 27: COOLEENLEMANE RIVER AND COBDUFF

An easy walk into the increasing remote, narrow and splendid valley of the Coomeenlemane River ends with a steep climb through crags onto a high spur reaching Bantry Bay. On this spur underfoot conditions are dull but they are compensated for by excellent seaward and Beara-ward views.

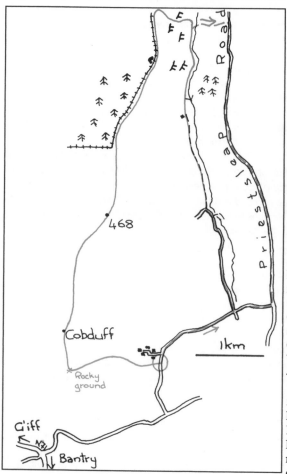

Getting There: Take the N71 from Glengarriff towards Bantry, turning left onto a minor road about 3 miles (5km) from the town at a sign stating 'walk 2'. Turn first left and park about a half-mile further on, just before fields on the left (GR 980557). If you have two cars you can make a better circuit by leaving one car just after turning off the N71 where the minor road swings sharply right (about GR 966548), starting the walk at GR 980557.

Walking Time: 4.5 hours (distance 13km, climb 550m).

Difficulties: None.

Map: Sheet 85.

Route: A slog on road to start. Walk onward from the

parking place, turn first left after about 15 minutes and walk to the end of the road. Specifically, cross a bridge near its end, pass by another bridge on the right which serves a house and swing left, onto what is now a track. Just before the track swings left again, turn right off it onto a minor track heading north.

You are now facing directly into the valley of the Cooleenlemane River, and a lovely valley it is. Walk to a shed where the clear track ends, and continue on an intermittent one northwards, crossing rough fields and meeting the occasional stone ruin, an unhappy reminder of tragic days in the past. Next you come abreast of groups of stately pines high on the right, standing below a minor road running by Priests Leap.

With these pines finally behind you there is a steep climb around boulders and crags and beside the occasional cascade to reach the upper valley. This is a more remote and wild version of the lower one, with great crags and steep slopes around the head of the valley and only the Priests Leap road high on the right offering any indication of civilisation.

Walk to nearly the end of the valley and then climb to the crest of the spur on the left, which ends 4km south at Cobduff. Though it is impossible to give an exact route it should be easy to avoid crags and the occasional slab. You will know for sure that you are on the crest of the spur because there is a fence running right down it: turn left to follow it. If you have ascended to the crest roughly where I think you should you will shortly come to a banana-shaped lake just over the fence. This will tell you exactly where you are, but it's all a bit academic since the fence has to be followed for miles; its purpose soon becomes evident as there are young trees beyond it a short distance below the lake. As already stated the underfoot conditions are far from memorable, but the views, especially west to the cone of Sugarloaf and the contrasting plateau of Hungry Hill are some consolation.

Eventually the fence swings away downhill and a modest climb to pt 468m follows. Beyond it take care, by swinging left, to follow the high ground ending at Cobduff (over 370m) and not that ending at pt 330m. Cobduff, a rather dumpy and shapeless affair, nevertheless offers a wide panorama, with the landward views still excellent and the seaward ones even better than before.

You can descend south from Cobduff for a few hundred metres (distance, not height) and if you have only one car turn east here at about a tiny area of high, rocky ground directly across your route (if you have a second car you will know to simply continue south over rough grazing ground to hit the road). Eastward will take you down through lines of slabs and then past a bulge of cultivated land on the left directly to your car.

Easy Variation: This gives you most of the highlights of the main route. Park at Millbig Bridge (GR 991564). Take the main route as far as the head of the Cooleenlemane Valley and then climb right to the Priests Leap road. Walk back to the start from here - it is easy to figure out the route from a road map. The walking time is 3.25 hours (distance 10km, climb 350m). ■

ROUTE 28: THE BUNSHEELIN CIRCUIT

North of Ballingeary the fertile basin of the Bunsheelin river is overlooked by modest cliffs and crags on two sides and by bland hillside to the north-east at Mweelin. Not the most dramatic of scenery but if you are in the area this easy walk is worth doing.

Getting There: From Ballingeary (GR 1567) take the road signposted 'Maghcromtha 17' (this is the Irish for Macroom and the sign is seemingly designed to deter non-Irish-speaking tourists, ie the vast majority). Drive onward for 1.1 miles (1.8km) to turn left at the second of two closely spaced junctions and turn right immediately. Continue onward at the sign 'cul de sac' and park at the plentiful waste ground at a fork about a half-mile (1km) farther on (GR 127698). **Buses:** 230, 255.

Walking Time: 4 hours (distance 12km, climb 520m).

Map: Both sheets 79 and 85 with awkward changeovers.

Difficulties: Rough ground to start with navigation generally easy.

Route: Take the road heading roughly west to turn left onto the second turning on that side. (This junction features a car wreck slowly integrating itself into the hedgerow on the corner. Don't worry that it may have disappeared by the time you come; it will still be there long after this book is out of print). Walk to the nearby farmhouse, and continue onward, southward and upward, now on a rough track until you are near the crest of the broad spur reaching west. Near its end, turn west off it to walk along the crest, with crags and the occasional stretch of cliff on the right bounding the Bunsheelin valley and should you care to look, unnaturally green fields on the left.

At the end of the westward-running spur you are into soft, undulating country. From here it is worthwhile walking south-west on a there-and-back to Coom-ataggart. The summit (about 530m) is topped by a tall, slender cairn and from it you can see the sharp cone of Mullaghanattin over to the west, the serrated line of the Reeks to its right, the plateau of Mangerton to the north-west and the unmistakable Paps to the north. All this and much of Gougane Barra close to the south.

Retrace your steps north-east to pass over onto sheet 79 at about GR 105700. Here, with crags and cliffs overlooking the Bunsheelin valley close by on the right you should come to a fence with a gate (use it) and a few minutes later reach a rudimentary track (2 hours). Watch out carefully for it is by no means obvious at this point. A turn right onto it gives a pleasant walk right back to the start. A turn left, as you will see to your horror, would offer only endless square miles of rolling, tedious bogland stretching away to infinity.

From the track head north-east over Lackabaun (472m), cliffs still on the right. After it you will see bog-workings lies ahead, unfortunately looking all too like a building site from a distance. Before you reach it however, you will drop into a narrow steep-sided gully - a surprising feature in a generally bland landscape.

Having negotiated the gully, and it may present a little difficulty, follow a fence on the right initially north-east - it forms the border of the bog-workings. Where the fence swings right (east) you might consider walking onward a few hundred metres to view a tiny wooded corrie and a large expanse of hilly country to the

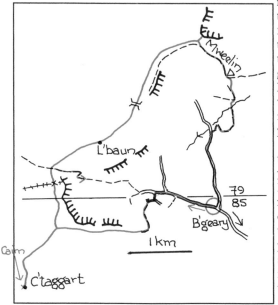

north. After that retrace your steps to the fence, cross it and take to a track, at this point traversing the undistinguished shoulder that is Mweelin (487m), whose formal summit is marked by a trig pillar just off the track.

Keep on the track until, just past the pillar, you cross a gate. Here leave the track to head roughly south-wards downhill, thus picking up another track improbably, but correctly shown on the map as an isolated zig-zag. Where the 'zig' hairpins to the first 'zag' leave this

track and head directly downhill for 100m or so through a field to *almost* reach yet another track, this one heading south.

Note that 'almost'. To reach the track you have to cross a deep-set stream, so it might be with some relief that you finally reach this track and easy walking. Simply take the track down to tarmac, turn left onto it and walk over 2km back to the start. ∎

ROUTE 29: GOUGANE BARRA

A scenic lake featuring a tiny church on a minute peninsula with woods, rugged mountains and cliffs penning it in on most sides, Gougane Barra is chocolate-box top country. This route gives good views with rocky terrain to start and good views and much boggier terrain to end.

Getting There: The start is 20 miles (32km) west of Macroom and also 20 miles east of Glengarriff. From *Macroom* take the N22 *east* for a short distance, here turn right onto the R584, turn right to Gougane Barra (well signposted) after passing through Ballingeary. From *Glengarriff* take the N71 towards Bantry, turn left onto the R584, branch left at Kealkill to keep on the R584, drive through the Pass of Keimaneigh and turn left shortly after. Park around the church (GR 092659). **Bus:** 255.

Walking Time: 4.5 hours (distance 13km, climb 580m).

Difficulties: The boggy ground has been mentioned. Navigation is quite demanding in bad visibility. There are a number of small landmarks on the route. If you lose them you could find yourself in quite featureless terrain with your way to lower ground blocked, especially on the northern side of the lake by small, irregular but nonetheless impassable cliffs and crags.

Map: Sheet 85.

Route: From the church walk onward taking the first turn left beside toilets modelled, for reasons unknown to me, on an African hut. Keep to this track for about 10 minutes by which time you will have passed a small field on the right. Shortly after the track heads predominently east and disobligingly downhill. Leave it about here and head uphill and south-west heading towards Foilastookeen, which is far from a distinct peak, though impressive cliffs fall on its north-west side, a good indication of your position.

The first landmark lies ahead: a fence corner at about GR 077641. Follow the branch running roughly west to pass a small lake (unnamed on the map), a larger lake (Lough Namrat on the map, though this sounds so un-Irish that it may be an anagram of Tramna or even Tarman - who knows what subtle joke the OS may intend) and finally a still larger one, Lough Fada.

At Lough Fada the fence ends so a compass bearing is necessary to find Lough Glas perched close by on the plateau to the north-west and incidentally the highest point of the day. From about here the mighty line of the Reeks to the west are prominent with, much nearer at hand the imposing Caoinkeen cliffs (route 26). Rocks disappear for a while as you push north-west from Lough

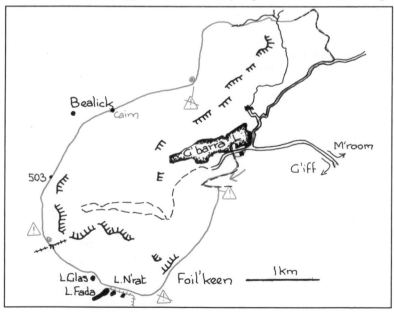

Glas, aiming for a tiny circular lake at a distinct low point. Just before it you will cross a fence (use the stile here) and, at 2 hours into the walk, you can decide whether to go on or retreat - and let's face it you have walked the more interesting half of the route.

If homeward bound take the deep gully on the right after crossing the stile; this will take you to the valley floor and a road. If you want to go on, head north into slabs, pass the indistinct pt 503m and then head north-east over boggy ground to reach the more easterly of the two 'summits' of Bealick (535m), distinguished only because it has an obvious cairn, the only obvious one on the route.

From Bealick head for another tiny circular lake to the north-east, passing through boggy country though with a few mighty slabs to add a bit of colour. This lake, a trifle nondescript though it is, is the key to the next leg, a contorted one designed to avoid cliffs to its east and south-east.

Walk north from the lake across bogland for about 10 minutes until faced by rockier rising ground. Turn east here to descend by a pleasant stream, a tributary of the Owennashrone River, or a little imaginatively perhaps, a source of the River Lee. Cross a soggy, tussocky area where several such tributaries are gathering, the idea here being to reach a track heading uphill on the far side. Once on the track, simply follow it down to tarmac, turn right here to take a meandering course through upland fields. At the bottom of this road, and now you are close to Gougane Barra Lake, turn left and right for the nearby start. ∎

ROUTE 30: MULLAGHMESHA

Not an area of high mountains, with Mullaghmesha itself not reaching 500m but, with lower country and the ocean all around, giving great views. Much tough ground underfoot which can be avoided on the short variation.

Getting There: The start is in the hamlet of Castledonovan (GR 1149) about 9 miles (15km) east of Bantry. To get there from the town take the road inland from its central open area, at its end fork right into William Street and continue straight ahead into Chapel Street. After 2 miles (3km) fork left at the sign 'Dunmanway 29km' and continue straight ahead to Castledonovan, parking on the main road south of the ruined castle, where there is plenty of space.

Walking Time: 4.25 hours (distance 13km, climb 580m), though the variation cuts this by about half.

Difficulties: There is lots of high grass, particularly on the second part of the route, though most of this can be avoided on the variation. Navigation is easy.

Map: Sheet 85.

Route: Take the road towards the castle making sure it (the road) is the right one, that which will leave the castle on your left. After over 1km steadily uphill pass a plant nursery and shortly after cross a gate on the right onto a track in open country. Take it uphill into an upland valley alongside a considerable stream on the right. Still on the track, ford a narrow tributary and walk onward to the track's nearby end at a contraption for holding sheep-feed.

From here walk through rough upland fields to a similar contraption uphill a few hundred metres away to the east at the end of a similar track. Walk north for a hundred metres or so to reach a narrow stream bounded by grazing land on the right and rough fields on the left. Follow the stream's bank uphill to its source in wet bogland and from there climb east through rocky outcrops to pt 509m, topped by a battered trig pillar. The summit commands a wide panorama of mountain, lowland and littoral, the latter stretching away to south and east, though the masts on nearby Nowen Hill detract a little from the view.

From pt 509m descend west to another boggy col and ascend from here to an undulating rocky ridge, which has no clear summit. As you descend make sure you continue west to the crest of a road, and not south-west, whither another bulge of high ground also ends on the road. 'Road' may be a misnomer however as this is a barely motorable route through remote and scenic country.

You might like to call it a day here as the terrain from here on is more difficult. If so simply turn left and walk directly back to the start. If you want to go on head west uphill through long tussocks keeping forest down on the right and a sturdy fence on the left (the ground is easier on its right). At length you will reach the summit of Mullaghmesha (494m) which has a tiny cairn set in bogland. The reward for your considerable efforts so far are a splendid panorama with Bantry Bay sheltering Whiddy Island particularly evident to the west.

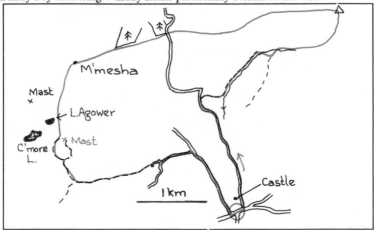

From here walk south, still impeded by tussocks. As you descend head for the left-most of two masts, one on each side of Lough Agower, which together with the larger Coomanore Lough shelter on the gently sloping moorland hereabouts. You will pick up a track here heading south and then east and pass a really monstrous boulder which looks set to tip over onto the track and if you are particularly unlucky, onto you. Incidentally look out for the fuschia along here, bordering the stream and later the road: it is most impressive.

You will meet tarmac at the highest farmhouse, and just beyond it at the second, turn left. All you have to do now is turn right at the next junction and with the castle now prominent ahead, walk the kilometre or so back to the start.∎